A MEMOIR

Finding My Way

COTEAU BOOKS

A MEMOIR

Finding My Way

LOIS SIMMIE

Edited by dee Hobsbon Smith
Book designed by Jamie Olson
Typeset by Susan Buck
Printed and bound in Canada

Library and Archives Canada Cataloguing in Publication

Title: Finding my way : a memoir / Lois Simmie.
Names: Simmie, Lois, 1932- author.
Identifiers: Canadiana (print) 20190127295 | Canadiana (ebook) 20190127325 | ISBN 9781550507935
(softcover) | ISBN 9781550507942 (PDF) | ISBN 9781550507959 (HTML) | ISBN 9781550507966 (Kindle)
Subjects: LCSH: Simmie, Lois, 1932- | LCSH: Simmie, Lois, 1932-—Family. | LCSH: Women authors,
    Canadian—Biography. | CSH: Authors, Canadian (English)—Biography.
Classification: LCC PS8587.I314 Z46 2019 | DDC C818/.5403—dc23

10 9 8 7 6 5 4 3 2

COTEAU
BOOKS

2517 Victoria Avenue
Regina, Saskatchewan
Canada S4P 0T2
www.coteaubooks.com

Available in Canada from:
Publishers Group Canada
2440 Viking Way
Richmond, British Columbia
Canada V6V 1N2

Coteau Books gratefully acknowledges the financial support of its publishing program by: the Saskatchewan Arts Board, The Canada Council for the Arts, the Government of Saskatchewan through Creative Saskatchewan, the City of Regina. We further acknowledge the [financial] support of the Government of Canada. Nous reconnaissons l'appui [financier] du gouvernement du Canada.

In loving memory of my parents,
Edwin Morris and Bessie Margaret Binns.

And for Anne and Scott and Daniel.

I think you must remember that a writer is a simple-minded person to begin with and go on that basis. He's not a great mind, he's not a great thinker, he's not a great philosopher. He's a storyteller.

—Erskine Caldwell

Mervin

My parents as newlyweds . Cavalier, 1926.

Pyramid

In an upstairs room with a slant roof a man is building a pyramid. The pyramid is constructed of toilet paper rolls on the foot of a double bed. The rolls are individually wrapped.

A girl about two and a half years old watches, hugging herself with excitement.

When the last roll tops the pyramid, the man sits on the bed, leaning against the wall, his long legs stretched out.

The girl scrambles up on the bed and runs down it, kicking the pyramid with her bare foot. White rolls fill the sunny air and she falls back down, laughing. Laughing and laughing.

The man laughs too, getting up to build another pyramid.

The house is in Mervin, Saskatchewan.

The year is 1934.

The man is my father.

The girl is me.

This is my story.

Glimpses

I do have distinct memories of kicking the toilet paper pyramid and laughing with my dad, but between that experience and learning to read I have only glimpses, kind of like driving on a remote road at night and seeing the odd sign flash by. I have no idea why there was such a long gap after such a vivid memory.

Glimpse:
My mother hanging clothes on the clothesline. The sunny, windy day, the billowing sheets whiter than the puffy white clouds, my dad's long underwear dancing, the wet legs snapping rhythmically, our dresses, stockings, underwear, all surging on the line, trying desperately to fly.

Prince, the Prossers' dog, sleeping next door, starts to bark as soon as he hears the clothesline creaking, and at the sight of the strange flying objects he begins to howl. He is obviously terrified, or in dire pain, and before long Mrs. Prosser calls him in to put him out of his misery. Sorry Mrs. Binns, she calls.

I knew, watching my mother take something from the wicker basket, give it a shake, clamp it onto the line with the wooden clothespins, shove the line down, over and over in a kind of rhythm, that she liked doing it, that it made her happy.

Glimpse:
Sitting on a stool beside the long narrow kitchen table with the tin top, watching my mother mix a chocolate cake. Her handing me the delicious brown mixture on a spoon. It fascinates me, seeing the ingredients coming together in the big tan-coloured mixing bowl with a raised flower on it.

Glimpse:
Sitting outside our bedroom door – mine and Betty's – watching Mom dip a sponge into a tin of pinkish-orange paint to make a pattern on the bedroom floor, earlier painted a bluish grey.

She had a wide creative streak, and was always painting or papering something. She papered the living room in a fern pattern, not green, but a warm orange brown. I loved that. I think I got my love of warm colours from her.

Glimpse:
Walking along the wooden sidewalk with my dad, talking and talking, as I was prone to do. He always listened. Picking a leaf off the caragana hedge, rolling it in my fingers, still talking. Something making me look at the leaf which is not a leaf but a caterpillar, screaming and throwing it onto the boardwalk, my dad laughing.

Glimpse:
Helping Dad plant the garden. Holding the stick with the string tied onto it, also tied to a stick at the other side of the garden. Watching him hoe a little ditch along the string, him putting some peas in my hand and showing me how far apart to put them in the ditch. Putting them in so carefully, if two were too close together, moving one over a bit.
Good job, he says, and I feel proud.

Glimpse:
Dad teaching me how to polish shoes. Being shocked when he spits on the toes of his dress shoes. Telling me about stands where he lived in the States, where men, mostly black men, would polish your shoes while you sat down and waited. You paid them, and it was a full-time job for lots of people there. Him talking quite a lot about Kentucky, where he came from, a long way south in the United States.

Once, when I was older, reading something about a city in the U.S, and asking Dad, Did they have people with shoeshine stands in Chickago? Where? he said. I was feeling quite sophisticated that I knew about such a place as Chickago. Oh, he said, yes, they do, and that place is pronounced Chicago.

I remember also thinking for a long time that the word "misled" was pronounced mizzeled. I still think it works better. It has a kind of weaselly sound that goes with being misled.

Glimpse:
Standing in the front yard in a new dress, beside Betty in her new dress that I liked better than mine. It is the first day of school and Mom is doing something with my hair. I'm not excited, I feel trepidatious. What will school be like? Will I like Miss Thompson?

I feel like I have to go to the toilet but I've just gone. You'll like it, Betty says. But what does she know, she's in grade five.

Crime Doesn't Pay

Playing in a sand pile with a boy, his name was Henry I think, behind his house, which was behind the barber shop. Maybe his dad was the barber.

We didn't have a sandbox and it was fun, the sand kind of damp so you could make shapes with it. He had a yellow shovel and I was using the other one, a nice red one. I really liked that shovel. He also had a truck you could fill up with sand and another thing that scooped up sand and dumped it out, but I was happy with the red shovel. I really, really liked it, it was shiny and fit in my hand so nice.

I must have absconded with the shovel when he was in the house. I knew it was wrong, but reasoned that Henry had enough to play with without the red shovel.

Before long I heard the phone ring inside the house and my mother came out looking for me.

Did you take Henry's sand shovel, Loey?

No answer.

Well, did you?

Yes, but he had two.

That has nothing to do with it. It wasn't yours. Where is it?

I reached around behind the water barrel and handed it to her.

No, she said. *You* are going to carry it to Henry's house right now, and you are going to give it back and say you're sorry. And I'm going with you. I'm ashamed of you and you've embarrassed me.

This wasn't good. It got worse.

You're going to say you're sorry to Henry's mother too, and if you ever take anything again that isn't yours, you will get a spanking.

That was really harsh. And it didn't sound fair but it didn't seem like a good time to say so.

It was awful. There we stood. Henry and his mother facing me and my mother, as if we were going to play some kind of game. Or dance.

My face burned and I wanted to cry but didn't.

I'm sorry, I blurted out, handing the shovel to Henry.

You're sorry about what? asked my mother.

I'm sorry I took your shovel. Mumbled.

You're sorry you what? she said again. Henry's mother was starting to look sorry for me.

I'm sorry I *stole* your shovel. Bursting into tears.

Crying and running isn't easy to do, but you can if you have to.

Mom stayed to visit and have a cup of tea with Henry's mother. And Henry played in his sandbox, with his dump truck full of sand and the thing that scooped up sand and dumped it out, and a yellow shovel and a red one.

My mother's lesson has stayed with me, except for swiping Royal Bank pens, and those little pencils by the bulk nuts at Safeway that are so good for crossword puzzles, and a scarf I took once at the Bus Depot when going through a terrible time. It was an ugly beige, not very clean scarf and for some reason I wanted it, *yearned* for it, actually. You can't, I lectured, and went home without it. After an hour or so I went back, it was still there and I took it. And never wore it.

Years later I read about Svend Robinson stealing a diamond ring for his boyfriend after being told the relationship was over. It was a big scandal. It was weird and so completely out of character. I understood it. But I don't understand it.

Falling in Love
With Words

I was in bed with the chicken pox. In my parents' bed, where we were allowed during convalescent stages of childhood diseases. It was there I suddenly learned to read. Out of the blue the words I had sounded out slowly all made sense. Suddenly *Dick ran fast. Mother and Jane baked a cake. Spot chased a ball.*

I couldn't believe it! I leapt to my feet and jumped up and down on the bed, screaming I can read! I can read! I can read! bringing my mother running upstairs. I can read! I yelled at her. Good heavens, I thought you were being murdered, she said, and stop jumping on the bed.

It was one of the most exciting and important days of my life. After all, what else would bring me so much pleasure through good times and bad for the rest of my life?

I became a voracious reader with, unfortunately, in

that little town with no library or facsimile thereof, not enough to read. Or books that stretch the mind of a child that age.

It was in school that I would fall in love with words. With sentences. With phrases. And with poetry. I was thrilled in grade four by a poem, "Wild Geese," by Martha Ostenso. I even liked her name, the rhythm of it. A real person called Martha who watched the geese, and sat down somewhere and wrote those words.

Something told the wild geese
It was time to go,
Though the fields lay golden,
Something whispered *snow.*

Something told the wild geese
It was time to fly;
Summer sun upon their wings,
Winter in their cry.

There was a middle verse I didn't like as well, so ignored it. I said that poem over and over to myself. The words excited me in a way I had never felt before. And they still come back when I hear geese overhead, gabbling like souls on judgement day. And so many other poems or bits of poems that wove themselves into the fabric of my life:

I must go down to the sea again to the lonely sea and the sky. There midnight's all aglimmer. The Arctic trails have their secret tales that could make your blood run cold.

Buffalo Bill rode a watersmooth silver stallion.

And who can forget poor jealous Tim the ostler: *His eyes were hollows of madness, his hair like moldy hay.* And "The Highwayman's" moody pictures – *The moon was a ghostly galleon, tossed upon cloudy seas.*

I hear those words on stormy nights. Wonderful words. I memorized poems for the sheer joy of just saying the words, and can still recite "The Cremation of Sam McGee", but nobody asks. My dad liked it, he was from Kentucky and loved a good story.

I read somewhere about a student who asked a writing prof if he thought she could become a writer, and he replied Well, I don't know. Do you like sentences? What a perfect answer. Like asking a painter if he likes paint.

Someone told me I said in public school I wanted to be a writer. I don't remember, but if true, it took me long enough.

But perhaps, that's not true, really. Reading voraciously for years, you somehow absorb what's good and reject what isn't. Some writers talk about the difficulty of finding their voice. When you're almost forty, it's part of you. I had also read library books on writing, everything they had. I highly recommend doing that if you're new at this. And I'd written the odd story and children's poem. I found one of my early stories recently – about a big paper clown that hung on my son Scott's bedroom wall, how it slips out in the dark one Halloween night – and I think with a bit of work it is publishable.

My first sight of a real library came when I attended the Saskatoon Business College, then called Success Business College. The principal, Mister Furse, was a neat, bustley man with a black mustache whose name inspired me to all kinds of silliness. The rhymes were irresistible; worse, nurse, hearse, first, cursed, etc. I'm afraid I was not one of their stellar students. They changed the name from Success Business College to Saskatoon Business College when I left.

Anyway, the old library, now the Saskatoon Club, Farley Mowatt's father was the head librarian then, I think. I got up the nerve to go in. Thousands of books, thousands and thousands of them. I didn't know how to look for a book. Not wanting to show my ignorance, I left and didn't go back. I was eighteen and felt the shame I would feel for years around educated people. It followed me all my life until I got up the courage to apply to the University of Saskatchewan as a mature student. I was always bad at math, going back to skipping grades in public school. I studied furiously – fractions, algebra, everything I could find from my kids' math texts – but it was hopeless.

The professor who read the exam results told me I had scored in the top two percent on the first part of the test. But I have to ask you a question, he said. My heart sank. Are you planning to study mathematics? he asked. And he laughed. That's when I started to believe I had a good mind. Well, half a one anyway. And over time that shame lessened.

Who knows what makes a writer? Curiosity, oh yes. Empathy, definitely. Something you're born with? Maybe. Steven King says it comes with the original package. But above all, love. Love for the tremendously exciting learning experience, love for your characters, for your readers, especially children, and a love of words and all the beautiful, exciting, unforgettable ways they can work together.

The Elevator

I don't know when I started to hang out at the grain elevator, where my dad was the Saskatchewan Wheat Pool agent, but I passed a classic scene from The Great Depression on my way there one day. Two men were sitting by a small fire close to the railroad station and I stopped to see what they were doing. They smiled through the dirt on their faces and said they were making coffee. When I told Dad he said they would be travelling by train, on the top of the train, or maybe in a boxcar, looking for work. Poor guys, he said. Mom was asked often for something to eat, since our house was close to the station. So, since the war ended the Depression in 1939, I must have been six or seven when the elevator became my favourite place.

I loved everything about the elevator: sitting and drawing at my dad's desk by the window, using indelible pencils and making copies with tracing paper sometimes; the engine chugging in the engine room a few steps down; the excitement of seeing a truck turning off the road onto the driveway and tearing out to see the truck box tip and the river of grain spilling through the metal grate in the floor. I liked wheat best. The sounds, the smells, the shouts, the dust, the clanking of the weigh scales. I loved it all. I liked the sound of men's voices, the laughter, the excitement in the air when the harvest was good, sometimes even a bumper crop after the long, dry years.

And sometimes Dad would take me up the lift, pulling us up on the small platform by a rope that dangled overhead, not an easy job. We would go all the way to the top, to the cupola. I remember the lumber smell and the sun slanting in from somewhere, the place loud with birds. I don't remember any dust, just the warm raw lumber walls, the airy feeling, and all the birds chirping madly at our rude intrusion. It was their place. It belonged to the birds.

I dream sometimes about going to the elevator after a long, dangerous trek and finding my dad still there in the office. It always makes me cry.

Bing

Bing was a big, black, beautiful Newfoundland dog and he had a harness that allowed him to pull my sister and me around on a sleigh. How we came to have Bing is a bit of a story.

A woman called Sally and her husband, Herman, lived on a farm a short distance from the town of Turtleford. Turtleford – Mervin's rich cousin – had a doctor, dentist, even a lawyer should you want to sue someone, a hospital, a drugstore and a newspaper publisher who put out the *Turtleford Sun* weekly. Ex-Turtlefordians still subscribe.

Sally and Herman had Bing. They also had a baby.

One winter day when Herman went over to his parents' farm a quarter mile away, Sally had an idea. It was so funny she couldn't resist it. But she should have.

She bundled up the baby till he was a round ball of baby inside a snowsuit. Then she called Bing and hooked up his harness to the sleigh. She put the baby on the sleigh and told Bing to go see Herman.

Go find Herman, she must have said.

And off he went.

A frantic Bing pulling an empty sleigh arrived at the parents' farm, barking hysterically for Herman and racing back the way he'd come, Herman and the sleigh in tow.

A short distance from Herman's farm was a clump of bushes surrounded by hectic sleigh and dog tracks, and inside the bush was the baby, unharmed. The snow showed evidence of Bing's heroic, impossible attempts to bunt the baby back onto the sleigh. I'm not sure but I think that baby was a girl. Maybe nothing in life surprised her after that.

Herman arrived home with the baby and the news that Bing was going to find a home elsewhere. Perhaps he suggested that Sally do likewise, I don't know. At the very least, he said, she didn't deserve Bing after putting the poor dog through such a traumatic ordeal. I think he let her keep the baby.

Herman was a friend of my parents' friends, Askan and Eva von Holwede, and Sally was Auntie Eva's sister. Uncle Askan said Sally was silly enough to do anything. They asked if we might like to take Bing

Visiting Uncle Askan in the hospital as an adult, I wondered who the flaming-red-haired visitor was, and the big-haired blonde who looked like her sister the next day. That was Sally, Uncle Askan said. I thought you knew.

We had Bing for two or three years and we loved him, my sister and I. He delighted in taking us for rides. He was wonderful to cuddle up to on the floor as we listened to Sunday night shows on the living room radio. And Bing loved us back.

But my father, who kept falling in holes that Bing dug around the outside of the house, got upset and gave him, without even discussing it, to our cousins. It was awful. When we all played outside after supper it was Margaret and Jeannie who called Bing home with them.

My sister and I never could understand how our kind dad could do something so hurtful. Why couldn't he have given Bing to someone we didn't even know? And it wasn't as if we had a beautiful yard. As we said every time we talked about it years later – we didn't even have any grass.

We got a dog who in no way replaced Bing, a little Pomeranian we called Teddy. We never grew to love Teddy, or at least I didn't, I was still heartbroken about losing Bing. I can't even remember how or why Teddy died but I know my mother, who had become more attached to him, really missed him.

Around the same time we had a white cat that was killed by a train, not the only pet in town to meet that fate. White cats are often blind. Deaf too, I guess, if you can't hear a train coming. Or feel it coming. For some unknown reason the railroad tracks were in some way attractive to wandering pets. And kids.

We had some adventures with Bing when we stayed at the grandparents' farm, not all of them good.

We also had a grey cat, Tommy, eventually called Old Tom, and he was our only pet after the little dog. I loved that cat with all my heart.

When I met Got To Go, the big grey cat who lived at the Sylvia Hotel in Vancouver, he was pretty much the image of Old Tom. Maybe that's what prompted me to write three children's books about him.

Once my grandson Isaac said, If there is a heaven –

he was a doubter very young – what do you think would be there?

Cats and dogs and books, I said. Algonquin Park, my son Scott said.

Showoff. A whole park.

The Farm

The J.R. Thomson farm, forty miles from North Battleford and a quarter-mile from Cavalier – just a railroad station and a small store – was a beautiful place. The home of my maternal grandparents, John and Annie Thomson, who left Minto, North Dakota, and Owen Sound to settle on a quarter section of the most productive land in the province, which would gradually expand to two quarters and then to three.

The house was a handsome two-storey. John Thomson had built the same house for his wife in Owen Sound, and Annie didn't want to leave it to be a pioneer in the middle of the Saskatchewan prairie. But my great-grandfather, Alex Thomson, had settled and worked some land near Leith, Ontario, and Grandpa had chosen the prairies for his own adventure.

The Thomsons had two boys, Jim and Bert, along on the long trek, and completed the family in Saskatchewan with a daughter, Bessie, born after the house was built. John had promised Annie that he would build the identical house, not likely much comfort to her on a long, long, difficult journey with two small children. A man bound for the same area remembers seeing her cooking near a railroad track somewhere on that odyssey. They were living in a tent.

The last part of the journey was in a Red River cart with the children, dark, skinny Jim beside her and blond, curly-haired Bert on her lap, when they ran over a nest of snakes, whipping around the wheels, terrifying her.

She was a strong woman, though, once sharing a seat with a woman on the Ferris wheel at the Seattle World's Fair. The gigantic wheel stopped when their seat was at the very top and the woman went out of her mind with fear and tried to climb out. My grandmother threw her long skirt over the woman's head and held her tight until they were down. That first year, they lived in a sod house on the property, but my grandfather, true to his word, built her the house she loved at that spot on the prairie.

It was a wonderful house.

It had a large dining room, with a window seat looking out at a large honeysuckle tree, whose fragrance filled the room. In that window seat storage I saw newspapers with a story of a woman murdered by her Mounted Police husband. Many, many years later I would research and write a book about that story, *The Secret Lives of Sgt. John Wilson*, which won a national prize.

Beautiful polished-wood sliding doors opened onto a parlour, with a large stained-glass window.

My only interest in that room was the tall oak desk with the beveled-glass bookcase on one side and a desk which opened up on the other by a kind of drawbridge becoming a writing surface. Several cubbyholes kept track of the business of farming.

A book called *The Titanic* was in the bookcase. There were pictures of the unsinkable ship, outside and inside, and pictures of the people who went down when it sank. An illustration of people in the freezing water holding onto whatever would support them, weeping, screaming, as the band played "Nearer My God To Thee." And suddenly not, as the great prow lifted out of water and it began its decent. Survivors have told of the terrible loud, haunting sound that went up from people in the water and on deck when the ship slid beneath the water. I would take the book upstairs, through their large, airy bedroom to the balcony and around to an ivy-covered corner where, horrified and fascinated, I read it over and over.

Grandma's flowers bloomed everywhere and I've planted some of her favourites wherever I lived – red Maltese Cross, bachelor buttons, daisies, poppies, brown-eyed Susans. The tall spruce trees at the front and side gates were landmarks of the Thomson place.

We had some great family get-togethers there. My cousins and their parents, Uncle Bert and Aunt Annie Thomson. And when Uncle Jim, the romantic uncle, who had gone off to live in Seattle, was there, it was so special. I have a picture of him laughing inside a giant Redwood tree. He always wrote on the back of pictures – who the people were, where, and the date. And often a joke. I should have learned to do the same with mine.

We all took turns turning the ice cream maker. After supper we asked Uncle Jim to recite poems. Now I think of it, maybe that's where I got my early love of rhyming poetry. Uncle Jim was a real orator, bringing those stories to life – *Into the valley of death rode the six hundred...*

The spacious outhouse, painted white with blue trim inside and out, had a high window. I was constipated a lot when I was a kid, and Grandma would go with me and sit beside me on the large space between the toilet holes, which had lids. She would hold my hand and talk, or we would look at the outdated Eaton's catalogue, and it helped.

But the most interesting building was Grandpa's workshop, which was full of unnamable stuff. We kids would put our fingers under the vice, and another kid would crank the vice down until we screamed and begged for our lives. Good guys/bad guys, played out over and over.

Harvey, the hired man, lived in a cottage across the road, his dog Rex chasing us, his black horse in a corral. We'd hang over the corral fence. I was scared of that horse but when cousin Marg bet I wouldn't go in and lick the salt lick, I did. And nearly had a heart attack hurling myself at the fence when the horse snorted. Marg had to pull me over. I think it impressed her, though. She was bigger than Jeannie and me and could hit a ball from the back of our garage in town all the way to the railroad tracks.

Grandpa chewed tobacco and would often send us to Cavalier to buy a plug of Club. I can still feel the hot, velvety road under my bare feet, puffing up between my toes. The telephone wires buzzing. We'd say it was Grandma and her neighbour, Mrs. Finley, on the phone, and we'd imitate Mrs. Finley. *Heel heel apenamy*, she would always say, rocking back in the chair with her palms in the air preparing to slap her knees at the story. We always wondered what she was saying.

Their neighbours down the road the other way were the Hayeses, from England. Grandpa had buffalo-hide robes, which he called the buffaloes, for when they had go somewhere in the dead of winter. Billy Hayes and Grandpa were planning such a trip, and talking to Billy on the phone Grandpa said, What do you think, Billy, should we take the buffaloes? And Billy would say, in his Yorkie accent, Oh no, I think just the ordin'ry 'orses.

Grandpa's obituary mentioned his sense of humour and a neighbour stopping to say John R's garden seemed to be doing well, and John R saying, oh it's wonderful, the potatoes are almost as big as marbles. I don't remember Grandpa ever laughing but he probably did when we left.

Sometimes Betty and I would stay with them, and if our cousins were there to play with I was happy, but if they weren't I got homesick. Betty, four years older, was no fun to be with – she was happy baking cookies with Grandma. I was terribly lonely for my mother, which was odd since I spent more time with Dad, but it was her I missed with such a fierce longing when I was away, as if I was never going to see her again. A portrait of her hung in the grandparents' big bedroom, her wavy hair falling over one side of her forehead. She was beautiful.

Nights were especially bad – moths bumping the screen, Finleys' dog barking in the distance, the grandfather clock downstairs softly bonging the hours and half-hours.

And it still hurts me to say this – after my grandparents moved to Mervin to be close to us, and my parents were still trying to think of what to do with all of those things in the house, a neighbour who had moved to Edmonton to open an antique store backed a huge truck up to the door and stole everything. Even my mother's picture. Even the *Titanic* book. They stole our past and I will never forgive them.

But I have the memories.

Sleepwalking

My sister Betty walked in her sleep.

A morning sound during that time was Dad lifting the wood door over the stairwell. This strange addition to our house was made to prevent Betty falling down the stairs while sleepwalking. She was about ten at the time. The door was raised and lowered by a leather strap handle and made a distinctive groaning sound when it was raised. As if it was too early to get up. It was so heavy only Dad could lift it. In the winter the upstairs was always cold at night, and with the advent of the sleepwalking contraption it was even more so.

I don't know what nudged her into getting out of bed in the middle of the night and walking. Where was she going, and why? My parents thought it must be precipitated by a dream but she could never remember the dream. Betty was a most unadventurous, good child, the one most mothers hope for, so these intrepid nighttime wanderings were surprising.

Perhaps her subconscious longed for more daring adventures. Most times Mom's maternal alarm jangled and Betty was found still upstairs, or downstairs but still inside. One night it failed and Betty was nowhere in the house.

In fact she was outside and already on the other side of the front gate, heading purposefully down the sidewalk. That was when the big wooden door was made. I can't remember how old she was when she stopped sleepwalking, but the door stayed there a couple of years or more.

Other morning sounds were: my dad clearing his throat downstairs, the clunk of the wood cookstove lids, the whoosh of the kindling being lit, and the lids banging into place. Then he started a fire in the living room heater, where we dressed in winter mornings for school. Later, coal would be added, and every so often he woke us up at night when he thought he detected coal gas. We would huddle under a blanket on the couch till he was sure it was safe. Dad was as obsessed about coal gas as Mom was about bedbugs.

After the morning fires were lit, Dad came upstairs to get us up. I hated getting out of bed in the winter, and if he didn't check I might have gone back to sleep.

One morning, dressing by the heater half asleep, I pulled on my long underwear with the back trapdoor – for convenience when going to the toilet – open, bent down to put on long stockings and plastered my bum on the heater. I think they heard me all the way to Main Street. I got to stay home because sitting down was not an option, nor was very much else. Lying face down on the bed, head hanging over, to read is really uncomfortable.

Here is my poem for children about Betty's night adventures:

Sleepwalking

There goes Betty Binns
Walking in her sleep;
Down the stairs, across the floor,
Down the hall and out the door,
Walking in her sleep.

There goes Betty Binns
Talking in her sleep;
She says hello to Mrs. Brown,
To Mr. Brown and Miss Brown,
Hello Hello to all the Browns
Talking in her sleep.

There goes Betty Binns
Walking in her sleep;
Up one street and down the other
Followed by her anxious mother,
(They told her not to stop her daughter
Walking in her sleep).

There goes Betty Binns
Walking in her sleep;
And Mr. Binns and Mrs. Binns
(With slippers on and hair in pins)
And Loey Binns and Teddy Binns
Walking after Betty Binns
Walking in her sleep.

(Teddy is the dog.)
I really wish I could include the illustration.

Sundays

I didn't like Sundays. Nothing to do, nowhere to go. My parents were not dedicated church goers. We all went only occasionally – Dad said he always felt like he was going to faint during the sermon – and I went to Sunday School but, like my parents, not religiously. Not a pun. The United Church was just across the street, the only church in town. Where did the Catholics go?

Sunday School was in the basement of the church, and all I remember about it was sticking felt Josephs and Marys and other bible characters, felt trees, etc. onto a felt background to illustrate the bible story of the day. Thinking of Sunday School reminds me of a story a friend who had taught Sunday School told me. When she asked the kids to draw a picture of the bible story, one boy drew a picture of a very large, very long car, driven by a very large man in a hat. A man and woman sat in the back seat. When she asked him what it was a picture of, he said, as if she was a bit dim,

It's God driving Adam and Eve out of the garden.

I once memorized the books of the bible and was presented with a small bible. I still have it. If I had two nickels for collection I'd often keep one to get candy from the corner store everyone called the Chinaman's. I can't remember his name but he was very thin and tall for a Chinese man or maybe that's because we were kids. He had a lovely nature. If you went in with a friend or two or three, and did a lot of giggling and deciding what to buy, he would just smile and say, *gulls have loss to talk abow.*

The church reminds me of the town undertaker, a tall, thin man with a problem that gave him a Monty Pythonesque walk. One leg went straight ahead and the other made a large circular swoop, as if it was a lot longer than the other one and constantly threw him off balance. He dressed in black and wore a black hat, and would arrive with a coffin on a flatbed trailer pulled by a black horse. My sister could imitate him to a tee, and she probably wasn't the only one in town. It gave me laughing fits every time,

He was creepy and maybe we made fun of him because the whole idea scared the hell out of us, the thought of a dead person in there. Someone must have helped him carry the coffin into the church but I never saw that, I only saw him going with that swooping gait along the sidewalk, and moving one leg by hand up the church steps.

I suppose anything, even church, or the undertaker's appearance, would help shorten the interminable Sundays. The elevator was closed. There was no train on Sunday. You didn't even play with your friends that much on Sunday, maybe their parents told them to stay home for a change.

If another kid showed up we usually went over to the railroad track to see how far you could walk on a rail without falling off. I always fell off first. The same discussion would usually come up about when people in the trains used the toilet, where did the stuff go? Straight through onto the tracks, we knew that, although no solid evidence ever showed up.

Once I remember being with some older kids who put a penny on the track for the train, soon coming, to flatten. We were too close to the tracks when the train racketed past. They laughed when the engineer shook his fist at us, but I was terrified. And ashamed.

Swinging on the front gate in that silent little town – even the town looked bored stiff on Sunday – I knew there must be places where Sundays were a lot more interesting. Wondered where. And how.

But Sundays have never become more appealing anywhere. And long weekends back when all the stores closed and the whole city had that empty, spooky look, like a plague had killed everyone overnight, that was having two bloody Sundays in a row.

You also find out as an adult that people alone on weekends become more aware that the whole world is walking arm in arm, living full, exciting lives. Everyone but you. I've been there too. Lots of us have.

It didn't change when I fell in love with God at age fifteen at church camp at Turtle Lake, insisted on being baptized so I could join the little Anglican Church in Livelong, and sang in the choir there.

Once church was over, Sunday was still there.

Dad's Girl

From the time I can remember I liked being outside and I liked doing things with my dad. When he chopped wood, I carried it into the kitchen and put it in the large, rectangular box beside the cookstove. The box was painted white, and had a lid. It was a great place to sit when you needed to warm up.

Something I've wondered about. We know about the dangers of asbestos, mesothelioma causing the deaths of so many who worked with it. What I don't understand is that we had a large sheet of asbestos on the wall right behind the cookstove, to insulate the wall from the heat. How come we didn't seem to come to any harm from having it there, year after year, exposed to heat? I've talked to friends who grew up in those times and places and they say the same thing. Raw asbestos in the open, not insulated behind walls. No problems. I remember Dad stressing never touch it but thought no more about it. If someone knows the answer to that, I'd be interested to hear it.

We got our drinking water from the town well close to our house and I'd go with Dad and carry a pail of water – or more like half a pailful – home. The pump handle had to be primed and that took longer some times than others.

Dad taught me how to identify weeds and I enjoyed pulling them after a good rain.

It was exciting to see something you'd planted break through the surface. I could identify everything we grew, and liked to tell people what they were, though my friends weren't impressed.

Dad took me to visit Ivan Slane, a bachelor who lived about a block from our place. Ivan was a town character – one of many – and in the summer you'd see him outside a lot. He was a tall, rather oddly built man, jutting out around his hips in big black pants with suspenders. He wore a grape basket on his head in the summer. He had a colourful 'flower bed' he had made from shiplap. Ivan's flowers had four petals, all bright colours, tall green stems and two long green leaves. Ivan planted them in front of his house. I see their imitators in garden stores now, and bought some once, thinking of Ivan.

The first time Dad took me to Ivan's, there was a good baking aroma in his big kitchen-everything-else room. Well, he did have a separate bedroom but it must have been very small. He told me where to sit and I looked around, intrigued. Ivan and Dad always had lots to talk about and I looked to my heart's content, until a huge black spider spiraled down beside me and I leapt screaming out of the chair to their great amusement. The spider was Ivan's handi-work and looked very real at first sight, but how he got it to zip down when he was sitting across the room was a mystery.

An almost-life-sized Kodak camera cardboard

cutout of a pretty, smiling, woman stood beside his stove. Ivan had tied a frilly apron around her waist. He called her his wife. His real wife had died a long time ago. He was making dog-legs, he told me, and they were almost done. Dog-legs?

The dog-legs were delicious cookies, cut out any old way, all kinds of shapes, which struck me as more fun than making them all the same with a cookie cutter. I think Ivan and I were kindred spirits. After that visit, I would drop in to talk to Ivan every now and then, sometimes with Dad, sometimes not.

He was such a smart, creative man, who had lived an adventurous life, panning for gold during the Alaska Gold Rush, working in the far north. He was an inventive photographer and showed me pictures of three Ivans sitting around a table playing poker. Time-lapse photography, he told me, and explained how that worked. I liked the way he talked to me like I was just another adult person. I was about eleven.

He had a two-storey table he'd made, the second storey a small round shelf in the middle with salt, pepper, sugar, mustard and other things he used a lot. He could spin it around so whatever he needed came to him.

Years later, the late great poet Anne Szumigalski said to me that we all have two ages. There's your chronological age, she said, and then there's your real age. You're eight, she said. How did you know that, I answered, how old are you? I'm four, Anne said.

I think Ivan was ten. An inquisitive, very smart ten.

Dad knew a couple of other bachelors he liked to visit and I'd sometimes go along. Usually on a Sunday and, since I hated Sundays, I was glad of any distraction. Mom stayed home making Sunday supper. One of Mom's complaints about Dad had to do with going shopping to North Battleford. Mom had an itinerary and was looking forward to shopping. Your dad stopped on the sidewalk every five minutes to talk to somebody, she always said when they came home. He was a talker. I am too.

The bachelors we visited had dogs so I could go outside and throw sticks or a ball for them, and I was intrigued by some of the old things in their house and around their place, and how they seemed to have everything they needed within reach. Once we went to visit a man who was lying on a cot with his leg in splints. That was interesting. He said his leg was broken and he'd put the splints – two boards – on himself. Dad did some things for him, helping him use the bedpan while I was outside and made him something to eat. Another bachelor looked in on him from time to time. His leg healed just fine.

Dad, having come from a city, Hopkinsville, in Kentucky, tried to show me glimpses of a larger world. He took me to the station to see the silk train go by at dusk. It was a sleek, dark, fast train, and quiet, all the windows covered with red blinds. And he told me about silk, how it was made with silk worms, and had come from India, and had travelled something called The Silk Road, carried by camels sometimes. The train was going east to Montreal, he said, maybe New York. In the animal world, that train would be a cougar.

Once he got me up early to go watch a visiting fair set up tents. The laughing, brown-skinned people didn't look like Mervin people, and somehow you knew looking at them laughing and shouting to each other that they didn't have boring Sundays. A couple of them waved to us, or called something at Dad.

We went to the Thunderchild Reserve a couple of times and took part in their Sun Dances. It was fun, holding hands and dancing in a circle to the beat of drums. There was a high wooden stanchion where coloured fabrics – were some of them garments? – fluttered in the wind. The people were welcoming – Dad knew some of the men – and there was a lot of laughter. Native people laugh a lot, and sometimes they don't have much to laugh about. I admire that.

At the North Battleford Fair one year, I was ten or eleven, Dad took me into a sideshow tent to see the Fat Lady who sat, like an island, in a sea of lapping fat. She had bright red lipstick and smoked with a cigarette holder and had a lot of yellow hair, probably a wig. She winked at Dad and said something that made him laugh.

The Midget was so small it was unbelievable, dressed in a little striped suit and tie with tiny brown oxfords, and smoking a small cigar. His voice was high and I couldn't understand what he said. There was the Tallest Man in the World, it hurt my neck trying to see his face, and also someone with too many arms or legs, I forget which.

My mother was shocked when I told her where we'd been and the Fat Lady winking at Dad. She said he probably imagined it. And I suppose it wasn't appropriate but I had enjoyed it. We both had.

The Playhouse

I don't know when the playhouse appeared, perhaps before my folks moved to Mervin. It was built in the ell between the back porch and the house, and probably Betty played in it before I laid claim to that great piece of real estate. My best friend Joyce Faber and I, and a couple of other kids, practically grew up in that playhouse. And on top of it, it was where The Great Experiment's endless variations took place.

I envied my friends who had more people in their families. Joyce was so lucky. She had an older sister, Anne, older brothers Hank, Walt, Jack, and Semon, and a younger brother, George. Her family was Dutch. Mrs. Faber gave me homemade bread with sugar sprinkled on top and I think of her when I still have that once in a while. She was so nice. Mister Faber was a big man, or that's how I remember him, and he would give me liver sausage on bread, and say, You're so skinny, doesn't your mother feed you? I was shy around Mister Faber and didn't know how to answer that, but I loved the liver sausage. Once he did the most amazing thing. He climbed on the table, lit a match and blew fire halfway across the room.

Mrs. Faber showed Joyce and me how to Dutch-fold sheets off the clothesline. I showed it to my daughter once to see if I still remembered how, and I did. Dutch folds have no edges.

Hank came home from the war with a gas mask, and we used it once by having George, who was quite small, put it on and jump up out of a pile of tires. Kids had to pay a penny to see the elephant, which some claimed – they of little faith and some knowledge of animal anatomy – that you couldn't get an elephant in there, but they had to pay the penny anyway, to see what was in there. I don't think we gave George any of the money – performers didn't have a union yet. George also came in handy when you played house, he had to be the baby and sleep in the wagon. Sometimes we'd forget him and he actually did go to sleep.

The playhouse was great for playing house and putting on shows. We can claim, undoubtedly, that Joyce and I invented the first TV. *Coloured TV.* We cut a square the size of a colouring book page, out of a large box. Gluing the pages together side by side to tell a story, we wound them on two broomsticks and, one of us on each side, wound the pictures past the hole in the box while telling the accompanying story. Admission to that was a nickel. We knew we had a hit.

Most fervent was the ongoing Great Experiment of finding a way to fly. Like scientists everywhere we tirelessly pursued our goal. If we just got the right contraption we could drift down from the playhouse roof, instead of wearing permanent scabs on our knees and other extremities from not drifting. We just knew there must be a way, and that the prize was worth the pain.

Kites, umbrellas, large pieces of cardboard, an old sheet which required a pilot and copilot, yards and yards of brown paper begged from the huge roll in the elevator driveway were all tried. Every new idea had to be rushed from my house to Joyce's house on my bike, or from her house to mine for consultation. We never did drift down off the playhouse but it wasn't for lack of trying.

Here is my kids' poem about art imitating life.

Flying

I'm learning to fly and it's taking awhile
Though I'm ever so clever and versatile;
I jumped from the roof of my uncle's barn,
With Spiderman kites tied to my arms
It worked for a second, maybe three...
I hit a tree. And fell on a bee.

Then with Grandma's umbrella and big straw hat,
(Did you know my nose wasn't always flat?)
With helium balloons and my brother's flippers,
A circular skirt and bedroom slippers,
Fans on my hands and a hat on my head
I got mashed and smashed and almost dead.

But one of these days you'll look up high
And there I'll be, just soaring by.
'Cause I know if I try, if I really try,
If I really, really, really try...
I can fly.

Going to the Lake

I couldn't wait. Every day was hotter than the day before, and we were going to the lake for a *whole week*. We had been to Meota Lake for a day more than once, and I had splashed in the blessedly cool water, the ridged sand under my feet, but we'd never stayed long enough to learn to swim. Now we were going for a whole week and I could practice every day.

Dad's fishing pole leaned against the porch wall, Mom looked tired from all the cooking, baking and other preparations, and Betty had a new bathing suit. A whole week to tear down from the nice cabin we had rented and immerse myself in that cool lake water. I wanted to stay wet for a week.

We set off early in the morning – for once I didn't get carsick, Mom said maybe I was growing out of it – and arrived in time to unpack everything before we ate the sandwiches we'd brought. Then Mom set to cleaning the cabin, which she said was disgustingly dirty and didn't people have any respect for the people who came after, and no, I couldn't go swimming for an hour after we ate. With a promise not to go swimming I ran down to the beach. Bare feet and warm sand, heavenly, and there was no rule against wading. I was hoping for another girl to play with and maybe to be a friend but there was no one else on the beach or in the water.

I was happily splashing around and picking up interesting stones along the shoreline when an enormous woman in a bathing suit came walking down the path, across the sand, and into the water. When the water was up to her chest she launched herself out and began to swim. Holy cow, I'd never seen anybody actually swim and I watched her flip onto her back and float, just drifting along with only her nose and her big round stomach and toes sticking up. What was holding her up? She wasn't moving her arms or legs. What could be more wonderful than that, just lying in the water and looking up at the blue sky? Like the lake was a big, cool, comfy bed. I had to learn to do it.

I ran home to tell my parents. Dad was just getting ready to go fishing and Betty was in her new bathing suit helping Mom put our things away in the cupboards and drawers and make the beds. Dad asked if I wanted to go out in the boat but I wanted to go back to the beach and see if I could stay up in the water on my back. If a big lady like that could stay up on top of the water it should be a cinch for a skinny seven-year-old.

Not so. I tried and tried and tried but just kept getting a nose full of water every time. Trying to imitate her swimming was even worse, some noisy boys came down to the water and made fun of my attempts. Not any girls, but it was only the first day.

I could see Dad rowing in the small boat, quite far

out, and he looked kind of lonely out there. I seemed to know sometimes that he was lonely, maybe because his real home was in Kentucky.

When he came back from fishing we returned to the cabin together. Betty was reading a movie magazine in the shade. Since we never saw any movies in Mervin I couldn't see the attraction. She would soon be twelve but seemed even older, and wouldn't go to the beach or in the water though I nagged her to. Mom, who was always busy at home, sat outside behind the cabin too, with her coffee and a cigarette. Sometimes she read a *Liberty* magazine or a book while she smoked. I was never going to smoke.

I went to bed early and fell asleep thinking about how the next day I'd go to the beach early and practice all day. If the big lady came again maybe I could ask her how to do it.

I woke up to loud voices, wake up, get up, we have to get ready to go. Go? Go where? We have to go home. Why? And that's when I saw the bugs crawling up the wall beside the bed. A lot of them, trying to escape my mother's murderous intentions.

I had never seen my mother so upset, and so mad. She had always feared bedbugs like they were the plague and would tell me if I played with kids who had them – everyone seemed to know who they were – I was not to go in their house.

Covered only with goosebumps, I watched from a wooden chair as Mom and Dad packed up food and dishes, emptied drawers and went over every single item with all the lights on and a flashlight, turning shirts and pants inside out, the pockets, too. Betty, covered in a big towel, told me to stop crying, but I couldn't.

It was worse outside, still naked, shivering and itchy all over as they hung the sheets and blankets on a clothesline behind the cabin and Dad went over every inch of them with the flashlight, his face eerily lit from below. Finally Mom put a dress on my shaking frame and told Betty and me to wait in the car where it was marginally warmer. Betty fell asleep but I couldn't. It was starting to get light out.

I could see the lake from the road as we drove away.

Going to the Dentist

There was no dentist in Mervin, as there was no doctor, hospital or drugstore. When we needed to go to the dentist we went to Turtleford.

My mother and my Aunt Annie Thomson both drove, and smoked, which caused me no end of embarrassment, though they probably weren't the only ones. I didn't mind driving with my mother, though any trip farther than ten miles made me carsick no matter who was driving. Aunt Annie drove like a bat out of hell. Or twenty-five miles an hour in an old car could feel like that.

Jeannie and I had dental appointments and Aunt Annie drove us to Turtleford. We sat in the back seat with the windows down as the old car rattled and banged over the potholed gravel road, the two of us hanging out the windows so as not to miss anything... crows on the fenceposts, cows in the fields, the bridge by Proctors' farm, horses. Jeannie, always braver than I was, hung much farther out her window. Suddenly she was gone.

Jeannie's gone! I screamed at Aunt Annie, who didn't hear me for all the other racket. Jeannie fell out! I yelled. Yelled again, and again, smoke from her cigarette blowing back in my face, finally grabbing Aunt Annie on the shoulder. Screaming in her ear, *Jeannie fell out! Way back there!*

Aunt Annie threw her cigarette out the window saying, Oh for heaven's sake, you kids, or something of that nature and I clutched the back of the front seat in terror as she executed a dangerously fast U turn and we went tearing back.

Jeannie was in the ditch, picking flowers. We weren't even late for our appointments.

After we moved to Livelong, we went by train to a shaky old dentist in North Battleford, a long, enjoyable trip on the way there, not so much on the way home sometimes. On one such errand, the freezing didn't take and the dentist pulled both my wisdom teeth without freezing. My mother said she heard me screaming from the waiting room. I think they heard me on Main Street.

I was a teenager the night my mother came home on the train after having all her teeth pulled. Mom was a stoic, but that night she cried and cried. The thought of losing all your teeth was so awful and I felt terrible for her but didn't know how to comfort her. We were not a demonstrative family. And then of course she would have to take that hours-long train ride back with no teeth to get the new false ones.

Betty, shortly after she was married at nineteen, was pressured by a dentist on I-don't-know-what pretext to have all her top teeth pulled, and grieved that loss all her life. She was nervous and shy and probably couldn't bring herself to stop him. She thinks it was for the gold tooth in the back of her mouth. Dad had wanted each of us to have a gold tooth, though I don't remember it being done and totally forgot I had it till a dentist mentioned it years later. I still don't understand why Dad wanted that.

For some people back then it was almost a rite of passage to have all their teeth removed in their youth. I suppose the parents were convinced by the idea of no more tooth problems. Or maybe the dentist just wanted the money, or, in my sister's case, the gold tooth.

The Binnses

My paternal grandfather, John Binns, gathered his seven children together at his handsome home near Hopkinsville, Kentucky, and announced that he was emigrating to a place called Saskatchewan somewhere in the middle of Canada, and whoever wanted to come along was welcome. Perhaps they were shocked, perhaps not. John Binns was a restless man. The Binnses had emigrated to Kentucky from the UK some years before and had established the successful Binns Milling Company in Cadiz, near Hopkinsville, providing employment for many in that beautiful part of the state.

They all came with him: Walter, the oldest son; Bert, next in line and the only one married, and his wife, Annie; four single daughters, Edith, Lizzie, Ruby and Kate; and the youngest son, nineteen-year-old Edwin, my father, who quit college to come. They came most of the way by train, with my dad looking after Grandpa's thoroughbred horses in the boxcar.

Grandpa Binns was probably writing poems on the journey. I have a small collection of his poems, many about Kentucky, and quite good for the style of the day.

A lot of Americans were joining immigrants from the UK and Europe, lured by the Canadian government's promotional barrage about the true north strong and free. And some, like my family from Kentucky, must have had second thoughts when the true-north-strong-and-free winds blew in January. At any rate, they stayed. Well, most of them.

My grandfather settled just outside the village of Meota, which bordered a lovely lake where I would learn to float so many years later. Money seems to have been no object when he built another fine house, the first in the district to have running water and electricity. This house was about forty miles from the house of John Thomson, my other grandfather.

I'm not sure when my Grandfather Binns returned to Kentucky the first time, but he left most of his children in Canada.

This is how I remember them.

Uncle Bert and Aunt Annie in Edam, just a few miles from Mervin, were the relatives we saw most often. Uncle Bert and Dad both worked as Pool elevator agents.

I remember those Sunday arrivals at their tall house on the first street in Edam. Their little black dog, Bugs, went ballistic with joy at our arrival, tearing around and around the car and barking his head off as, with difficulty, we exited. Inside the house he tore maniacally up and down the steep stairs two or three times and ended his welcome by jumping all over us.

Uncle Bert was a sweet man who showed me different kinds of corn he was developing, I remember the cobs sprinkled with blue, and in some a kind of winey red. It was more than a hobby but I don't know if there is any Binns corn. Aunt Annie was the most southern of all my relations, her accent warm and kind of rhythmic, and she was a talker, a foil for my quiet Uncle Bert. I don't remember Betty being along on most of those trips. A teenager, probably.

They had two sons, my cousins Hubert and Maurice, both quite a lot older than us. Maurice was a pilot who flew at most of the fairs, doing tricks and taking people up for rides.

Once he landed in a field beside our house in Livelong, a most exciting event for us and for the town. He took Dad up for a ride and did a loop-the-loop. We could hear Ahhhhhhhh! – Dad's opinion – from the ground. Maurice took me up for the same experience. Having your stomach do the loop-the-loop is pretty interesting and I bit my tongue but remained silent. Fear paralysis.

My cousin Hubert looked like the actor Omar Sharif. Hubert ran a small grocery store in the town of Prince. Hubert was quiet, like Uncle Bert. He apparently fell in love with a married woman, and she with him. Her brothers, known to be thugs, came to the store one night and beat him mercilessly, blinding him in one eye.

Uncle Bert and Dad, both Pool elevator agents, had a lot to talk about – the grain business, the rest of the family, word from Kentucky – and my mother and Aunt Annie were close friends. Aunt Annie lived to be a hundred, such a rarity then that the whole town celebrated.

Aunt Annie always tried to find something for me to do, or read. A colouring book and crayons, the *National Geographic*, but the day often dragged, and I was ready to go home long before my parents.

Y'all come back now honey, Aunt Annie always said

as she hugged me goodbye.

Uncle Walter, a big, shy, slow-talking man, was the other family member we saw most often, at Meota, and Aunt Bessie.

Aunt Bessie had been a maid or housekeeper for someone in the district. She was short with a wild brown frizzle of hair and a Yorkshire accent. I remember her best sitting at the small kitchen table in a cloud of cigarette smoke rolling cigarettes with one of those early cigarette rollers. I can hear the chunking sound when she pushed the roller over and back and another cigarette popped out. They had only one child, my quiet cousin Ronnie, several years older than I was. They adored him.

Apart from Ronnie and cigarettes, Aunt Bessie had another love. Plants. Their small sitting room was a jungle. Tall plants filled the bay window, shutting out a lot of light. Plants, plants, everywhere. Crowded on tables. Gushing out of wicker planters. Set on the floor. Hanging from the ceiling. You were lucky to find a chair in there. I guess Uncle Walter was used to it.

My shy cousin Ronnie was killed in the war in Italy. It was a blow like no other. They never got over it.

In my teens, I spent quite a lot of time at Uncle Walter and Aunt Bessie's, and grew very fond of them. Of course I was also fond of lying around in the lake every day. The big woman who floated wasn't there any more. But the exciting Meota Pavilion dances were, where a guy called Donnie McAngus made jitterbugging feel like flying.

We rarely visited my Aunt Kate, who had married a man called Bartlett. He didn't care for the Binnses. I visited my cousin Bill Bartlett years later, a handsome, really nice man, who lived on a farm outside Victoria and who had a lot of beautiful, very-long-eared rabbits.

We would also go to see Dad's sister, Lizzie, who married a man from England and they farmed not far from Meota. She had only one arm, having fallen out of a high chair as a baby. Aunt Lizzie could peel potatoes faster with one hand than I ever could with two. Don't ask me how, even watching her I couldn't figure it out.

I had three cousins there: Kay, Walter and Harry. Aunt Lizzie's husband, John Kittle, was not a great visitor, and usually had some chore that needed attending to until we were almost ready to leave. Walter and Harry, university students in those days, were talented piano players. I always asked for "The Flight of the Bumble Bee," and they indulged me, though jazz was their passion.

Dad always wanted us to go to Kentucky. The summer of 1950, Kay and Betty and I would make a trip to Kentucky with Aunt Lizzie. We went by train through Manitoba after the disastrous Red River flood. On a bus later in that trip I was enjoying talking to the black woman beside me. The bus driver announced the Mason Dixon Line – Dad had told me about it – and she started gathering up her things. I have to go sit in the back now, she said. I'll go with you, I said. Oh, no, honey, I would get in trouble and so would you. My introduction to racial injustice. Whites Only drinking fountains. Whites Only restaurants. Whites Only washrooms. A consciousness-raising experience I'm glad to have had at that age. In the '60s I would watch the coverage of the young Freedom Riders and it all felt very familiar.

Two brothers, twins, who Aunt Lizzie had taught in her twenties, honoured her with a beautiful party at a *Gone With The Wind*-style southern mansion, or so it seemed to us, outside of Hopkinsville. At one point a very old woman saw twenty-two-year-old

Betty and cried Lizzie! I thought I'd never see you again! Betty was not delighted to see her old friend. We were shy, especially Betty, feeling our country bumpkinness and were mostly just overwhelmed and trying not to be seen on that occasion.

We went out to the Binns Milling Company at beautiful Cadiz, and saw the river and the gigantic overhanging tree Dad and other kids would swing from into the river. We did see both sides of Kentucky – *Gone With The Wind* and hillbilly yards full of old cars and furniture and dogs and people rocking on the porches. I'm reading a book about how many of them left to go west to try for a better life in Missouri, Arkansas and beyond, so many it was called "Hillbilly Highway." The found work and many prospered in these new environments, and, working hard, were able to join the middle class, but returned to Kentucky and family every chance they got.

Grandfather Binns's need for change took him back to Kentucky, or maybe it was the winters. I don't know if any of the children went back with him that time. I say that time because he moved back to Saskatchewan again, maybe because most of his family was here now. Eventually he went back to Kentucky to stay. He was getting older and Aunt Edith, the only daughter who hadn't married, went back to look after him until he died. Then she returned to her brothers and sisters in Saskatchewan.

Aunt Ruby had married late and happily, and lived in Turtleford with her nice widower husband. I was in Turtleford when I was fifteen and decided to go and visit them. As I approached on the leafy street I saw Aunt Ruby and Uncle Alfred smooching up a storm on their verandah. I was shocked, they were so old – in their fifties – and decided to visit another day. Sadly, Alfred died young, of a heart attack.

Ruby and Lizzie, both widows, and Aunt Edith, came to share a roomy apartment in North Battleford.

I was working in North Battleford and my parents living in Ruddell, a short drive away, where I last remember the aunts' Sunday visits. I can still see the three pairs of good shoes lined up in front of the couch, my mother toiling away in the kitchen, aromas of roast beef or chicken, apple pie, and one or other aunt would call, not quite loud enough to be heard, Can I help you, Bessie?

They would leave in a flurry of Bye bye Eds, Thank you Bessies, and waving arms as the grey Nash pulled away for the trip back. Dad would stand at the window and look at his watch. How long should we give them this time? he would say. And sure enough, in a matter of minutes the grey Nash was appearing around the corner, parking in front. Aunt Ruby would run in, Lizzie left her scarf, or Edith hasn't got her glasses, variations on the theme each time, and more Bye bye Eds, Thank you Bessies, and they were gone until next Sunday.

I have been ADD all my life. The whole damn family is. And it's not our fault.

Floating

I'm not sure if it was the year after the bedbugs at the lake that we went back again, or perhaps the one after that. I can't imagine anyone persuading Mom to go back at all. But apparently friends in Meota knew of a cabin rented by someone they knew, and we packed up again. By now Betty was a teenager, with boys on her mind, and she on theirs. She looked so pretty in her white bathing suit for tanning – she never went in the water – and wore her hair at the back in a snood with little green velvet bows. I had to laugh every time she said Have you seen my snood? I can't find my snood. Like it was a little animal. Smaller than a cat, I thought.

The cabin was nice, and clean as a whistle, Dad said. I wondered if the enormous lady who floated around the lake would be there, and if she was if I could get up the nerve to ask her to show me how. I headed down to the beach with the usual 'Don't-go-past-your-waist' warning. If I could float like that fat lady I wouldn't go real deep like she did – she could swim – but just float along close to shore. She hardly moved anything on her body, I remembered, at times kind of lazily using her arms to pull her along. I bet she could go to sleep doing that.

She wasn't there the first day. Maybe she moved away, I thought, since someone who could do what she did would surely be doing it every day. But the next day I was paddling around when she came walking down the path to the beach. She was even bigger than I remembered. Hello, she said, before walking into the water and when she was up to her chest she swam for a bit, straight out, then flipped over on her back and floated. I was going to be on the beach when she came back. *She had said hello.*

She finally came back and paused on the beach, shaking water out of her short hair and maybe her ears since they were submerged when she floated and she didn't wear a bathing cap. You're still here, she said. I nodded. You like the water? I love it. Good, she said, and then, Can you swim? No, I said, and when she turned to leave burst out, Couldyoushowmehowto-float? I said it so fast I wasn't sure she knew what I said.

Sure, she said, just like that. *Sure.* She asked my name, and said I'll see you tomorrow, Loey. Her name was Jenny. She said it just like that, My name is Jenny. I liked the way she said it, like it was okay, normal even, for me to call an adult by their first name. And I loved the name. Jenny.

As soon as she was out of sight I ran screaming all the way to the cabin. Mom said, What? Why are you screaming? They can hear you all over town.

I'm going to learn to float! She's going to show me how to float! My mother looked relieved. But not where it's too deep. No, she just floats in shallow water.

Which was a lie, of course, being how big she was,

she needed quite a bit of water to hold her up. But Mom hadn't seen her and didn't need to know that.

Jenny gave me my first lesson the next day. Just relax, she said, holding me horizontal with her big hands. Now put your head back in the water, a little bit lower, keep your stomach up, your legs just a little bit bent, like that, yes, that's good, that's really good. She had me just flutter my hands a bit. And she said I was doing really well.

Every day that week she was there. Now just move your arms slowly up and around and push the water – she would demonstrate – That's good, that's good, you keep practicing that, move your feet a little bit up and down, just a bit, and gradually she pulled away her hands from under me, one at a time, and I floated for a few seconds before I realized they were gone, and promptly sank.

By the end of the week I was floating by myself and Jenny went back to floating all over the lake. Mom said now she had to worry that I would get out too deep without knowing it, but Dad rowed around close to shore for the last two days we were there. I was floating in more ways than one. Something I'd dreamed about had come true.

I could lie in the water and look up at the blue and white sky, clouds floating, like me, while the water held me up, kind of like a friend. Like Jenny. Every day I was getting better. Dad was impressed. Mom was too, though she still thought I might go too deep. I think even Betty was, a little.

Maybe there would be a lake in Heaven, but for now heaven was doing this amazing thing.

Going to See the Queen

Get up. Get up. We're going to see the Queen. People always said that, going to see the Queen, like the King was not important.

The summer of 1939. It was all people talked about for months, King George and Queen Elizabeth were coming to Biggar, Saskatchewan. They were coming on a train that was taking them across the country, and we were going to Biggar to see them. We knew what they looked like, their picture in crowns and robes and rabbit fur was on the schoolroom wall, right above the blackboard. I don't know about other kids but I wasn't very excited about seeing them, maybe because I got car sick, and would have happily stayed in bed.

We were going with the Wylies. Mister Wylie, a friend of Dad's, ran the hardware store. One day Dad came home laughing. He had dropped in at the store on his way home from work and found Mister Wylie excited about some light bulbs he'd just got that were guaranteed unbreakable. Dad said he didn't believe they were unbreakable but Mister Wylie was convinced that they were. I'll prove it, he said and went and got his stepladder. He put a lightbulb on the floor and climbed up on the ladder and jumped on the lightbulb. It smashed to bits.

By seven o'clock we were all in Mister Wylie's car. We were going early so we could get a good spot to see the King and Queen. Mister and Mrs. Wylie and Dad in front; Jackie Wylie and Betty and me in the back with Mom in there somewhere, under me, I think. I was skinny and didn't weigh much.

Jackie Wylie was already fidgety. Jackie was all right but there was something wrong with his mind, and he had to have everything explained so often kids didn't really want to play with him. But he was okay, he wasn't mean or anything.

Mister Wylie couldn't get the car started. He tried two or three times. I guess she'll need to be cranked Ed, he said, and Dad got out and cranked and cranked till he got so hot he had to take off his jacket and have another go. Mom tried to roll down the window. That one sticks, Mister Wylie said. Finally, when Dad looked like he'd just run fifty miles, the engine started. We were away.

It was a long, long drive, never-ending it seemed, and it made me feel sleepy and sick at the same time. But we finally came to the sign. "BIGGAR SASKATCHEWAN," it said, like we might actually think we were in Newfoundland. It's too bad the present sign, "NEW YORK IS BIG BUT THIS IS BIGGAR," hadn't been thought of yet. Lots of people were already at the station and as soon as the car stopped Mom ran me behind the station and I threw up.

After standing there about an hour we heard the train whistle and it appeared in the distance with flags flying. We all had small Union Jacks and Dad had brought his Stars and Stripes, Old Glory he called it. The train slowed, slowed, and finally stopped with the ordinary-looking man and woman on a back platform right in front of the station. People waved flags and cheered. Dad waved both his flags and said the Queen had smiled at him. Mom said she had not, but it was possible since he was taller than the people in front and maybe she was amused by this lone American.

No crowns or rabbit fur anywhere. Just a sad looking man in a blue suit and the smiling woman in a big blue hat and a dress like my mother's Sunday and Ladies' Aid dress.

We ate the sandwiches Mom and Mrs. Wylie brought and got back in the car.

It wouldn't start. Dad got out to crank the car again and had to take off his jacket again. When he looked like he'd run another fifty, it started. It was odd they said, that it didn't start when it was warmed up by the drive.

Dad and Mister Wylie talked in the car about the King having a lot on his mind, people in England were afraid Adolf Hitler would start a war. It did not look good, they said. What would happen to them, I wondered. I felt sorry for the King.

Mom really liked the Queen's hat but Mrs. Wylie thought it was too big.

I said why didn't they have their crowns and rabbit fur.

In the noisy car, I heard Dad say from the front seat It's not rabbit fur. It's vermin. Of course, Dad actually said ermine, but that's not as interesting as vermin. Still, I learned something that day.

On the way home Jackie Wylie threw up on me.

The War/Maurice

The war broke out the September after our short lake holiday. I only knew Hitler was evil – a word I had only heard in Sunday School – but knew it was very very bad. Knew by the sound of the man's voice giving the war news on the radio – I can hear his voice still – knew by my parents' faces as they listened.

It was all the adults talked about, in the stores, the Chinese café, the lumberyard, on the street. Boys interminably played war. Toilet paper at the school was given out one or two squares at a time. Metal – iron, steel, tin – was desperately needed for the war and we kids were urged to gather as much as possible.

I don't think it was patriotism that urged my cousin Jeannie and me on, scouring alleys, dumps, our houses, everywhere until we had a wagon load. It was the money that was offered – so much a pound – Dad weighed contributions on the weigh scales at the elevator.

Finally, when we could pull no more even if we

could find any more we set off for the elevator. Partway there our wagon was hijacked by Carl Horner, the biggest meanest kid in town, and the money – our money – gone. You know how hard it is for kids to deal with injustice. That one was hard, but an early lesson that life was not always fair. The kid was a lot bigger and when you're a kid, big rules.

My cousin Maurice, a pilot, joined the air force as soon as war broke out. After some basic training he was commissioned as an officer because of his flying experience.

One night he came to say goodbye to the folks. When Dad opened the door and Maurice came in wearing his officer's uniform I knew it meant that he was going to war and might be killed and I couldn't stop looking at him. He was beautiful.

They had drinks – Maurice had brought a bottle of whisky. The occasion called for more than coffee or tea. Maurice and Dad were more like brothers than uncle and nephew. His father, Uncle Bert, was almost the oldest in the family of eight, and my dad was the youngest.

It was past my bedtime and I tried hard not to be noticed, but at some point Mom sent me up to bed. Certainly later than my usual bedtime but I didn't think about that, I was heartbroken. I tried but couldn't hear what they were saying from the top of the stairs. I wanted to look at this wonderful human being who was actually my cousin. Wanted to hear him talk. *My cousin.* Finally I went to bed to think about him going to war and it made me want to cry.

I heard someone coming up the stairs and there he was, in my room and sitting on the side of my bed, smiling at me. Talking to me. Just to me.

I don't remember much of what he said except to commiserate with me. Then he offered me a stick of

Juicy Fruit gum. I chewed happily while he talked. After a bit, another stick of gum. I happily chewed some more. The he said he had to go down and talk to Mom and Dad. Chew that gum, he said, till it's really sticky. Then stick it on the bedpost. It will upset your mom.

And he was gone. Off to war. I loved him from that moment on.

Maurice survived, and came back to flying jobs in the North.

A Visitor

One stormy winter day my father arrived home with a strange woman. A strange woman in a brown uniform. Her name was Mary Hudson. Some people in town, including us, had people in the Forces home for a weekend from North Battleford detachments. We'd had a nice man from the Air Force a couple of times, short and unassuming in his uniform; a paler blue, it seemed, than Maurice's uniform or maybe it was just him. Now here was a woman in an army uniform. I didn't even know women could join the army.

Dad took her coat and hat, shaking the snow from them, and introduced her to Mom. And to Betty and me. She was pretty. Black hair, bright red lipstick and a Betty Grable shape in her brown uniform. She was in the CWAC, the Canadian Women's Army Corps, and she could stay a few days if that was all right with my mother, who could hardly say no.

It snowed and blew for three days, as prairie blizzards did then. They played cards, the air was smoky

Betty, me and JoJo Hudson, son of the army woman. I am eight.

with her and Mom both smoking. Dad never did. Well, almost never. Every night after supper he would sit down to read a paper – *The Western Producer* and the *Family Herald* or a magazine, and smoke one cigarette with his coffee. I wish I'd been a smoker like him instead of a frazzled cigarette addict.

When Mom was cooking, Mary Hudson and my father would talk or play cards, just the two of them, and she looked at him a lot. I asked her what army women did, did they shoot Germans? and she laughed and told me a bit about things they did, office stuff, driving officers who for some reason didn't seem to know how to drive, and sometimes driving ambulances. Except for the ambulances, it sounded boring.

She went out with Dad when he shovelled snow and when we needed something at the store. She just needed a bit of air, she said, and by the third day my mother looked like she needed a lot of air without Mary Hudson in it.

I should take a moment to say that my father was an attractive man – tall and broad-shouldered, with a wonderful smile. He had a very slight Kentucky accent, and the natural charm of someone genuinely interested in other people. He liked women and women liked him – she was not the only woman to be smitten. She thanked us all when she left and hoped she would see us again. Shortly after the first visit, her photograph in uniform appeared on our piano. I didn't see why we had it there.

And come back she did, in fact she was the only one from North Battleford who did come. They went to dances, the three of them – she wore a red dress – and sometimes with a bachelor friend of Dad's. I saw her draw a line up the back of her bare legs to look like nylon stockings, all the nylon being used for parachutes at the time.

My parents started to argue in their bedroom. They did that sometimes, but their voices were raised now. Once when Mary Hudson came, she brought her son JoJo. JoJo was a bit older than Betty, twelve or thirteen, and he was all right. I didn't know she was married, so maybe she was divorced. Nobody in town was divorced.

Once when she came before Christmas she brought new dresses for Betty and me. I hated mine, itchy yellow plaid with black trim, which made me like Mary Hudson even less. We wore them to school – Mom said nobody should turn their noses up at new dresses – and walking to school Betty said we were not to say where we got them. She sounded like an adult telling me that. I was already feeling uncomfortable about Corporal Mary Hudson or whatever her army rank was, and being told not to tell where we got the dresses filled me with anxiety. It was like a family secret, which of course it was.

That was the beginning of my feeling anxious most of the time. I was anxious when she was there and when she was not, because nothing was the same. My parents didn't laugh or even talk much any more, and the arguments behind the door got longer and angrier. And they both looked sad. Dad, sitting in his wing chair in the evening smoking his solitary cigarette, and Mom reading on the couch or playing solitaire at the dining room table.

Spring came, and summer, and though Mary stopped coming, it still didn't feel good.

Then one day they said they were going on a holiday together, just Mom and Dad, to visit Dad's family in Kentucky. We were going to the farm until they came back. Mom asked us what we wanted them to bring us. Betty asked for a new dress, a blue dress with a frill. I asked for red sandals, I had seen a girl wearing them in North Battleford. Mom drew a pattern around my foot on paper, like we did when we ordered shoes from the catalogue. I asked Dad to bring me some blue grass.

We waved them off, the four of us, as they drove away, Dad's arm waving out the driver's window till they were out of sight, like someone needing help. Now I'm kind of amazed that they would undertake that long, long journey in a car, especially ours, which wasn't new and sometimes had to be fixed.

Time dragged while they were away, each day longer than the day before. What did it mean, this trip, were they trying to get along better? What would happen if they didn't? I moped around with no one to play with and nothing to do, except to sometimes play checkers with Grandpa, who got mad if he didn't win. Evenings were better – we played cards, or Parcheesi, which was all right when I wasn't Uncle Bert's partner. Shake a twelve. Shake a five.

And so the time came when they were on their way home. I tried to keep my fingers crossed for two days but couldn't and thought that would mean bad luck and it would be my fault. I couldn't get to sleep at night, hearing moths bumping against the screen, the Finleys' dog barking in the distance, the soft bonging of the grandfather clock downstairs.

One night we woke to their voices downstairs. We went to the head of the stairs and heard Mom talking about a black widow spider that they found in the car, just above her head. Scary. Come down, come down they called, and still I hesitated, afraid to know. Till Mom said, Come on, Loey, come and get your present, and I did.

Betty opened hers first, a wonderful blue dress with an enormous frill, and she ran off into the kitchen to try it on. While I was opening mine – a shoebox size package – she came back and twirled around in the dress, the skirt so full it touched each of us and fluttered the flame in the tall Aladdin lamp.

I pulled the tissue paper off of the first shoe. Shiny red straps, silver buckles catching the light. My heart beat faster as Mom slid it on my foot. Perfect, everyone said, and it was, my brown skin showing between the straps. I stood up, it still felt good. I pulled on the second one myself, trying to adjust it, trying and trying, but something was wrong. Mom pulled it off and looked at the two together. They were both for the same foot.

I would never forget it.

And Kentucky blue grass is not really blue, just a kind of greyish blue. Dad said it had faded some. But he remembered, that was important.

I don't know what eventually happened to the shoes after I hobbled around and got blisters. My mother must have disposed of them.

That night I think I knew my parents still weren't happy, but time went on that summer and nothing changed. Until one day at the farm.

The day I heard my mother and Betty talking in Grandma and Grandpa's big bedroom. I started to go and join them and just as I got to the partly open door I heard something that made me pause.

Just you and I are leaving? Betty sounded excited, and Mom said yes.

What about Loey? Betty asked.

Loey will live with your dad, Mom said. She didn't sound the least bit sorry.

I crept back down the hall, ran down the stairs and outside as fast as could. I ran crying. It was happening. We wouldn't be a family any more. And Mom didn't want me. The way she said it.

I don't remember where I hid first. I didn't want to

go back even when later I heard Dad calling me. And calling. And calling. And then everyone calling. I cried so hard I could barely see.

There were so many hiding places at the farm. Grandpa's workshop behind all the stuff he kept in there. The ice house. The wash house. The barn loft in the hay. The granary. And the other building that never really had a name. I ran from place to place when I heard Dad getting closer, and ended up, exhausted and still crying, in a small kind of playhouse that nestled in the trees on the way to the front gate. It was starting to get dark and that made everything worse. That's where he found me.

He didn't need to ask me what was wrong. I cried even harder when I saw him and it all poured out. They sounded like they were talking about Tommy, I told him. Our cat. He sat on a low stool with his elbows on his knees and his head bent and listened as I let out all the sadness and fear I'd been living with for so long and, finally exhausted beyond words, stopped. He didn't say anything, that I remember, just listened, and when I had calmed down a little he took my hand and said, all right, it's time to go now. And we walked back to the house.

My eyes were swollen shut. Grandma bathed and bathed them till I could see a bit. When I asked about them she said they were talking. And she rubbed my feet until I went to sleep.

Back home, summer ended and school began. Mary Hudson never came back again, and her picture disappeared from the piano. Years later I was looking for something in a drawer full of family pictures. Near the bottom lay her photo, glass broken. I don't know why my mother never threw it away.

Things gradually got better. I started spending quite a lot of time at the elevator. It seemed to help me.

Though I still had a kind of longing love for my mother, it felt almost normal again.

The war news on the radio became the most important time of the day. Everywhere people gathered around the radio at the same time. I knew Dad was thinking about Maurice flying big bombers over Germany every night.

Dad tried to join the forces. He belonged to the Battleford Light Infantry Reserve where the men in town trained, in case they were needed to go to war.

We were at the farm when he left to enlist and we waited there for him to come back, or to let us know if he wasn't coming back. It was finger-crossing time again. When he came back and said they wouldn't take him because he had a very slight limp from having polio as a child, he looked so disappointed that for a moment I wished he'd been accepted, but the flood of relief drowned it out immediately. Mom looked happy, too. And I started to believe it would be all right.

Note. Many years later I wrote the story "Red Shoes," which appeared in my short story collection *Pictures* published by Fifth House. Atlantic Films bought it for a short film, which won first prize at the Cincinnati Film Festival short film category and second prize at the Chicago Film Festival. It was submitted for an Oscar but it didn't win.

The father was played by the actor who is the father in *A Christmas Story*, the movie about the kid and the Red Ryder rifle. I try to watch it every Christmas.

Rheumatic Fever

So many teachers joined the forces during the war that the small, remote towns sometimes got the bad ones. One of them was our grade four teacher, whose name I have mercifully forgotten.

On the first day of school she ordered Walter Tesch to the blackboard. He complied as fast as he could but not fast enough for her and she hit him on the back with a yardstick. He had polio, you know, I piped up at this injustice. She turned and looked at me and I knew right then that grade four was going to be awful.

Worse than awful, as it turned out. I started faking sickness to stay home, but the pain in my stomach was real enough sometimes.

She also took a dislike to Jackie Saunders, the cute boy who sat behind me – I had a crush on him till he laid my scalp open with a metal-edged ruler – and we both solved our teacher problem the same way.

I don't know what pushed Jackie Saunders over the

edge – the way she liked to hit him, I suppose – but mine was a spelling test I got ninety-eight percent on, one wrong. She called me to the front, produced the strap and whacked my hands till they were fiery burning blobs on the end of my arms. I howled, screamed, blubbered. You're a good speller and should have got a hundred, she explained in a reasonable voice when she stopped, as if everybody knew that but me. I think my dad had a pointed word or two with her.

Shortly after, while riding a toboggan behind the delivery sleigh, something inside me shifted, like water rushing down a drain, and I kept falling down on the way home. I remember standing in the back porch unable to get out of my boots, let alone my snowsuit, my mother pulling off my jacket sleeves and my arms flopping down, wanting to lie down with my hot face on the wet, wood floor, my father carrying me up the stairs.

Remember being not in the bed I shared with Betty, but in the spare-room bed. Remember a strange, dark plasticine man who amazingly stretched up to the ceiling and down and sideways surrounded by a dancing orange light, my parents' receding and looming faces, garbled voices, the words, 'doctor,' 'delirious,' 'very sick'. I had rheumatic fever.

So, it turned out, did Jackie Saunders.

What followed made me wish I was back in grade four. I was consigned to the corner of my parents' bedroom in a strange white iron bed, and Miss Johnson, the town nurse, on doctor's orders, moved in. She slept in my parents' bed, about two feet away from mine.

The two worst things. As an addicted reader, not being allowed to read. It might hurt your heart, Miss Johnson said. She read aloud from the Bible, which was scarier than her, but not a lot. The other was not being allowed to have Tommy, my big grey cat, on the bed. I longed for his big warm body. Miss Johnson would not allow it, and when he came up meowing for me she screamed and chased him all the way downstairs.

I submitted to the daily wintergreen rubdowns – to this day the smell of wintergreen takes me back to that room – and all my joints being wrapped in itchy red flannel, but the sight of Miss Johnson coming in the door with a bedpan and a hot water bottle equipped with a long rubber hose made me scream and try to get away. My mother had to hold me or she wouldn't have managed it.

Every night Miss Johnson changed into her long nightgown in the closet, twisted her hair up in strips of paper, and stood looking out onto the street, her knobby little head outlined by the streetlight outside. She would sigh heavily, kneel down between our beds and say her prayers out loud, and they always ended the same. Please God, don't let Loey die in the night.

I didn't worry about dying, but worried a lot about the war coming to Canada, and how would I get away? Hearing the war news on downstairs, though I couldn't understand it, opened up a cold, empty space in my chest. Days dragged by, became weeks, became months. I spent a lot of the time facing the wall, away from Miss Johnson.

One day while Miss Johnson was out of the room, Tommy came in and jumped on my bed. But he didn't want to cuddle and, making a strange howling noise, he ran to the end of the bed, lifted his tail, and expelled a great tangled ball of worms. My screams brought her running with her arms full of sheets off the clothesline, and he shot off the bed and escaped by running under hers and away while I somehow lurched onto her bed. She screamed and ranted about the filthy cat. My mother ran in from the neighbours' and tried to calm this screeching madwoman who'd had enough of being shut up for months with a sick child she didn't like and who didn't like her.

Later she came up from dinner and slammed a bottle of rubbing alcohol onto the dresser spilling alcohol onto the almost new waterfall bedroom suite with its beautiful round mirror and a frieze of lighter wood leaves. Your father has quite a vein of sarcasm, she said. I didn't know what she meant, I'd never heard of that vein, or where it might be, but it sounded like my dad didn't like Miss Johnson either and that made me happy. My mother loved that suite and never forgave her for the damage.

Not long after that I was well enough for us to get rid of Nurse Johnson. My folks were almost as happy as I was. She'd had to eat all her meals with them and I'm sure she missed my mother's wonderful cooking when she left.

I remember them both supporting me and Betty looking on, smiling, as I got out of bed the first time on very shaky legs, my heart full of happiness.

Two things that still make me wonder.

How did Doctor Yaeger, the country doctor who rode down to Mervin from Turtleford on the railway jigger that winter night in answer to my parents' frantic call, know to diagnose me so promptly and accurately?

And how two picked-on kids from the same class got rheumatic fever, a not common non-communicable illness, at basically the same time?

Where are you, Jackie Saunders? I'd love to know how you're doing.

Livelong

The Move

Dad was going to run the Pool elevator in Livelong after years at the Mervin elevator. Two Mervin elevator fires, clearly arson, had been resolved, or resolved to be unresolved. Was it a farmer who felt unfairly treated or just a random act of someone who wanted some excitement? Suspicion had even fallen on Dad. In any case, agents were transferred from time to time and perhaps after the fires a move was wise. It had been a difficult time for him. The investigations. Suspicion. Gossip.

I remember the night of the first fire, the anti-sleepwalking door banging, my father shouting, Oh God, Oh God, running down the stairs, the back door slamming. Betty and I getting out of bed and looking out the window to where a strange reddish light lit the sky in the direction of the elevator. My mother sitting on the bed beside us until we fell asleep. And, when there was nothing left but ashes and charcoal, the strange sight of a little blonde girl from Mervin's biggest family, I don't remember her name, sitting every day in that big black circle, eating charcoal.

The moving-day drive from Mervin to Livelong when I was eleven feels like it happened last week, I so-vividly remember the unfamiliar scenes unfolding. The drive to Turtleford was one we'd made many times over the years for doctor and dentist appointments, drugstore needs, but from Turtleford on it was all new.

Snake Hill, just out of Turtleford, disappointingly snake-free; the rolling open country beyond. Every dip in the road opening out into an exciting new landscape. And the trees. Tall spruce and pine, trees almost absent in Mervin, anchored the land in every direction. Spotted birch groves like tall giraffe conventions, fluttering aspen, trees, trees everywhere. The landscape seemed to be saying, You are in a far more interesting place now, a more generous place, and it will be good. It enfolded and welcomed us. That drive, not much longer than an hour, if that, made the transformation all the more amazing.

As we got closer to Livelong the road dropped into an immense, very steep coulee, a valley with a long vista in both directions and one lonely house clinging to its slope. I remember that first cautious drive down into it, clutching the front seat in fear that the brakes might give way. Climbing the other side with the car straining mightily on the steep incline felt even scarier. The possibility of crashing backwards seemed even worse. There was nothing half so exotic as this in the vicinity of Mervin, the setting of which had become familiar to the point of boredom.

Dad was excited, not wanting us to miss anything. Close to the Livelong turnoff the land dropped away to the right, a wide area unlike the surrounding countryside and dotted with ponds. That area down there is called The Flats, he said. On the long straight road into Livelong he pointed out the farms tucked away in the rolling land, the fields, the duck-filled sloughs, everything. He was like a kid opening a beautiful new picture book, and I felt it too, the excitement. The pages yet to be opened.

You'll like it, Tommy, I said. Tommy, who wanted none of it, crouched on the back-seat floor.

It didn't occur to me until many years later but it was the new start we all needed. For my father, from the problems of the two elevator fires and investigations; for my mother from the memories, and no doubt gossip, about my father's infidelity, now a painful history; for my sister, who had been mercilessly bullied for years in school and after school by two nasty girls, Greta Clark and Betty Kirk, making her life a misery; and for me, coming to the end of a long convalescence from rheumatic fever and my constant worry about my parents splitting up. I felt the decision had been made to put that all behind them, which made me happy and excited about the move despite leaving my best friend Joyce and other friends, behind.

The Pool elevator cottage – cottage in name and size but not in charm – was situated on a treeless lot at the end of a street with a small stockyard across the road, where we would often hear Walter Hicks and a hired man shouting and branding cattle, the cows' indignant bellows of pain and helplessness. In the backyard was a small shed and, of course, the toilet, where Mom would again battle nature with frequent doses of lye.

The house was very small with not one redeeming feature, one small bedroom off the kitchen, small sitting room with a heavy green curtain partitioning off the second small bedroom, no hardwood, linoleum throughout. It was such a disappointment after our nice old two storey house in Mervin – I loved that house and so did my mother – that I'm surprised she didn't sit down and cry. She didn't, and I never heard her complain. With Betty's piano and a couch in the small front room there wasn't space for much more.

And, unbelievably, in 1943, there was no electricity. Dad pumping air into the gas lamps would always terrify me, but I was familiar with the kerosene lamps from Grandma carrying them up to bed when I stayed there. Dad tried to make it seem like an adventure, like camping. Mom was not excited.

More than anything, I missed the trees in our Mervin yard, the enormous poplars where I spent so much time climbing with friends or alone, retreating up there trying to figure out life and worrying because I'd stepped on a crack in the sidewalk and my mother had complained that her back hurt. I was intensely superstitious and, unfortunately, still am, although not quite as bad. A year or so earlier I would have missed the playhouse but I'd grown out of it by then.

But discovering the proximity of Turtle Lake – just five miles away – made up for a lot. No more boring hot summers with nothing to do. We had arrived at the best time of our lives together. In that small child's drawing of a house, we would become a family again.

Years later, I would write a poem about moving, for kids who had to leave a much-loved place: "How Do You Say Goodbye?"

How Do You Say Goodbye?

How do you say goodbye to a house
When you're moving forever on Saturday?
When you've lived there forever - seven years,
And no matter what, they won't let you stay.

How do you say goodbye to a room
With its just-right walls and corners and nooks?
With its Snoopy curtains, all faded and blue,
And shelves for your toys, and fishtank, and books.

How do you say goodbye to the tree
That grew up so tall by your bedroom window,
That dances its leaves on your yellow walls,
And lulls you to sleep whenever the wind blows?

How do you say goodbye to a street
Where you know all the hedges and places to hide,
The back alley gate where you broke your arm,
And the hill at the end where you used to slide?

I wish I could move this house and this tree -
This yard - this street - these swings;
My friends can all come and visit me,
    But how do you say goodbye to things?

Livelong School

I dreaded wearing those ugly, brown, old-lady oxfords on my first day of school in Livelong. I'd had to wear them after rheumatic fever and the doctor and my mother were adamant. I had to wear them a little while longer.

The grade five teacher, Miss McNab, was nice and tried to make me feel comfortable. I was embarrassed when she introduced me and I tried to look normal. Why is it so hard to look normal? You don't actually realize what that looks like until you try to look it.

That first recess I stood against the school wall, wishing there was something to hide my shoes behind but of course there wasn't, and the other kids didn't approach me. Maybe they didn't know what to say.

But it probably wasn't as long as it seemed before a cute dark-haired girl came over and said Hi, I'm Marina. My first friend in Livelong.

I'm Loey, I said. I was never called Lois until I left to go to business college in Saskatoon. Somehow it still doesn't feel like my name. When I talk to friends from back home they call me Loey and it still feels right.

I peeked at Marina's feet, and holy cow, she had on ugly brown oxfords. She had to wear them for some problem, weak ankles I think. So of course we bonded. Not that the other kids were wearing great shoes, and some of them wore brown oxfords too, but they didn't have old-lady heels like mine.

My mother was a wonderful cook and I always looked forward to going home for dinner at noon. The noon meal was always called dinner, and it was many adult years before I could call supper dinner without feeling like a phony. In that little town the only kids who had to bring lunch were the kids from the country. I went back to school after that first dinner break feeling much better. The ice was broken because I liked the teacher and had found a friend.

I soon got to know other girls: Josie Ferrari, a giggler; Marlys Christianson, with her almost-white Swedish hair; and Jean Nichols, who lived out of town and wasn't around as much as the others. Josie also left for home after school.

One day Miss McNab was talking to a grade seven boy, on the other side of the room. He was making a salt-and-flour map and I was intrigued, having never seen one.

You're doing a nice job, Daddy, she said.

Daddy? Could a kid be called Daddy? That was weird.

I asked Marina why he was called Daddy, bringing on one of our giggling fits. His name was Dante, Josie's brother, from a large Italian family that lived on a farm.

The leaves were still on the trees when Miss McNab started planning the Christmas concert. We began rehearsing in October. Miss McNab couldn't wait.

I was starting to love Miss McNab. She was a great teacher, and shared my love of poetry. She was as excited as we were about the Christmas concert. The best teachers – and writers, too, I think – still have a lot of the child in them.

The Mervin teachers – and not just the dragon we had in grade four but most of them – had been quite strict. I don't remember one ever laughing in the classroom but they must have. They didn't rule with an iron thumb – weird Stalinist-like expression – but viewed any disruptive behavior, like giggling, as a threat to be stomped out lest it lead to complete anarchy. I remember Miss Thomson from grades one and two, she had a very fishy smell, sometimes worse than others. She was the guardian of the toilet paper. When we needed to go we held up one or two fingers, to denote which job was imminent, and were given one or two squares of toilet paper. Paper was rationed because of the war and if we used all the toilet paper there would be none for the soldiers. Sitting in the toilet with one piece of toilet paper didn't help me feel patriotic.

At Livelong School we were all treated with respect, even affection. And Miss McNab laughed a lot.

I'm not sure now what we did that first year for the concert. But concert highlights over the years include all of us girls drifting around in long blue dresses singing "In My Sweet Little Alice Blue Gown," I still remember most of the words. Remember a very silly thing where we were savages in bathing suits with wild hair and face paint beating drums and singing bongo bongo bongo I don't want to leave the Congo. Political correctness was still a long way off. We practised and practised Christmas carols, Wally Harse beside me singing "Hark the Hairy Angels Sing" and smiling angelically when I got caught for laughing.

One of the acts in a later year was Donald Harley and the Flaming Torches.

Miss McNab told us to pull down the blinds on all the windows, we were going to see something exciting, and holy cow, was it ever. This was in our brand-new high school. We quieted down and Don came out of the cloakroom with two wooden clubs and when he got to the front he bowed and juggled them. We clapped and clapped. Then he lit them on fire.

He whirled them and twirled them and threw them up and caught them, one at a time and both together, and passed them behind his back and created fire patterns in the air as we screamed and clapped, it was so amazing and would electrify the Christmas concert audience. School was great.

And by spring I had grown out of old-lady shoes and didn't need them any more. It was all behind me. It was as if I left an unhappy time – rheumatic fever, worry about my parents – behind with those shoes.

A funny postscript about the shoes. Marina and I were goofing around at a rummage sale in the town hall, and I took them off to try on something else, and when I looked, they were gone. Oh, Mrs. Harse said, Jean Simmons bought those shoes, we didn't know they were yours. My mother insisted I go to her house and get them back.

Easier said than done. I had to work up my courage to go and ask, but finally knocked on the door. Come in, Jean called. She was sitting wearing my shoes smoking a cigarette and was not inclined to part with them.

Her husband, Charlie, the shoe repairman, came to see what the problem was. His shop was in the back of the house. He didn't help much, and I must have sat there more than half an hour before she reluctantly gave them back.

Jean was a collector. The walls of that little house were covered with clocks – clocks with pendulums, cuckoo clocks, a cat clock with a swinging tail, clocks of every description. Suddenly they all rang, chimed, whistled, bonged, and cuckooed at once, and I almost fell out of the chair.

Those were such good years, I even liked the small house, where we physically were together more, a plus for small houses. I would polish the wax Mom put on the linoleum floors by dancing around in a pair of Dad's wool socks to music on the radio. I felt closer to my mother after we moved and that made me happier than anything.

It wasn't just school. Livelong people were a whole lot more interesting than Mervin people. The town bordered miles of wild north country around Turtle Lake and beyond, where people who came into town for groceries and dances were fiercely independent and colourful.

There was Mike Denny, who came into town in the summer seated high in a buggy in a woman's print summer dress, a straw hat and work boots, his wife beside him. He said he didn't see why women should be the only comfortable people in the heat. My parents were friends of a Finnish farm family who invited them out for saunas and naked rolls in the snow. That shocked me.

Ivan Slane, our close neighbour, was a creative town character with an interesting past; Walter Hicks was a loud, big presence in town, always looking for the next big thing, or terrorizing cattle across the road; our neighbours, the Doolittles, had eight kids. Nobody in Mervin had eight kids. There was a mad preacher at a little church by Turtle Lake.

We had found a home there. And my dad, being an

American from Kentucky, added another coloured thread to the mosaic. He loved the people there, we all did, and I think they loved us back.

Me with Tommy

The Doolittles

Next door to us in Livelong was a house even smaller than ours, where the Halls lived.

Mister Hall liked to fix things, or he liked to think he liked to fix things, since their yard was filled with things that needed fixing – cars or parts of cars, bicycles, unidentifiable things, a washing machine once. I don't remember Mister Hall out in the yard tinkering, not for any length of time, not long enough to actually fix something. I feel a definite kinship with Mister Hall, who obviously suffered from procrastination. He couldn't help it.

The Halls had a small daughter and a baby. But their attractions paled beside the Doolittles, who lived in the big unpainted two-storey house next to theirs. The Doolittles had eight kids and I still remember their names from the oldest to the youngest: Robert and Jenny and Joyce and Larry, and Margaret and Ruby and Annie and Gary. I think I've remembered their names all these years because of the rhythm and rhyme.

By the time we moved to Livelong, Betty was already fifteen and I had just turned eleven, so we didn't do much together except spend time at our grandparents' farm in the summer. Maybe that's why I enjoyed it so much when she made chocolate fudge at home and we all listened to the radio Sunday night, *Amos'n'Andy, Edgar Bergen and Charlie McCarthy, The Shadow Knows*. I would sit on the floor between Mom's knees and she brushed my hair a hundred strokes or more. I loved that feeling of closeness with my mother, but all of us.

I tried to look interested when Betty thrilled to Frank Sinatra on the radio but I couldn't understand what all the fuss was about.

So I spent a lot of time at the Doolittles where there was never a dull moment and Mrs. Doolittle paid no more attention to me than if I belonged there. I think she thought I did sometimes. I wasn't a particular friend with one of the sisters but just liked being with them all. Sometimes their cousins were there, too, which was even more fun. Mister Doolittle worked on the railroad and I remember him coming home from work with his lunch pail. He was a quiet, good-natured man and he needed to be. I have always wished I belonged to a big family, and still do.

Robert Doolittle was two or three years older than I was and one day when I was thirteen and was walking home from my friend Marina's house, Robert stopped me in front of their house and gave me a valentine present. A square one, nicely wrapped. I don't remember if he said anything besides Here. I looked at their house and I think the seven other kids were lined up in the window watching this rite of passage. I ran home in a fit of embarrassment and threw the present in the corner of the back porch hard enough to break whatever was inside, and went inside.

Mom said What did you throw in the porch? and Why is your face so red? and I said, Nothing. And, it is not.

Mom retrieved it and opened it when I wouldn't. It was a box of stationery. Poor Robert, she said.

I think Robert was already in trouble, or about to be, there was a rumour that he had poisoned Jimmy White's, the barber's, drinking water, and he was sent to a reform school for a while.

His cousin, Percy Harse, is a friend of mine and when I told him recently about Robert's present, Percy said, He probably stole it. He also said that Robert was so light-fingered he was known as Robber Doolittle. If I'd known that then, I might have found Robert more interesting.

Years later, when I was working in Calgary as a file clerk at California Standard Oil, I was with some friends who had come up with the insane idea of going to swim in the river at night. I did my share of stupid things but drew the line at that. On our way there was a bulletin on the car radio about a horrific car crash that killed the Doolittle parents, some of their children and two friends – girls Lyla and Verna Opperman. Robert's child and the youngest child, Gary Doolittle, were the only survivors. As the friends went swimming, I sat in the car remembering the Doolittles, and suddenly feeling very homesick.

I thought of those days and wrote a poem some boy or girl with a small family might relate to.

The Neighbours

The neighbours are exciting to visit,
There's three of us and eleven of them;
The neighbours are exquisite to visit,

I was there last night and I'm going again.

Sammy has rabbits and Barry has pigeons,
Tammy has guppies and mice;
Their dog's having puppies, I hardly can wait
Gil ate a goldfish and said it was nice.
Simon is digging a hole to China,
He's worked on it all week long;
His father drove in from the alley last night
And stopped halfway to Hong Kong.
Jonathan's band is rocking
With the speakers amplifying;
The twins are covered with little red spots,
Jackie got smacked for lying.
The baby is getting her baby teeth,
Joshua's getting expelled;
The neighbour's father smokes a lot
Their mother drinks muscatel.
Their mother is having a basement sale
The week before Halloween;
She sticking price tags on rabbits and kids
And looking kind of mean.

No one's going to buy them I hope,
It just wouldn't be the same;
The neighbours are exquisite to visit
I was there last night and I'm going again.

Hollywood

There was no theatre in Mervin so I'm puzzled about where I saw a movie there. Somewhere on Main Street. The movie was *The Hound of the Baskervilles*.

I don't think I was there with Betty or a friend but surely must have been. I was launched into a strange, dark, foreboding world. Riveted to the chair, covered in goosebumps every time that enormous hound howled. Bayed, a better word. The sound of fear.

When it finally ended, I bolted for home, my heart racing, down the alleys because it was faster. Almost there, I tripped on something and fell behind the Prossers' yard, next to ours. A loud howl. The Hound, coming for me. Prince, the German shepherd, aka The Hound. He howled and howled as I crawled, my legs too shaky to run, to our backyard and home.

Eons later, after an Old Bags Club dinner at my place, we talked about the first movie we'd ever seen. Everyone had been very frightened by what they saw. That was interesting. One was about a clown, I remember.

In Livelong, there was a movie every Friday in the town hall. No projection room there, Frank Harse, the postmaster with the kindest brown eyes, I'm sorry nothing for you today, ran the film from a raised platform at the back of the town hall. When latecomers passed through the beam they were told to sit down!

Livelong movies were mostly westerns. Roy Rogers, Gene Autry and their sidekicks, galloped madly to get the bad guys. Once in a while there was a comedy.

My first date was with Wally Harse, who asked me to go to the show. When we got to the hall and the pay window Wally, overcome with embarrassment, paid and dashed in to sit with the boys. I sat with Jean and Charlie Simmons, Jean's little white dog – she was never without it – attached to her chest. It slept but growled once at something. I don't remember the movie. Wally walked me home.

One movie that was such a complete surprise, a shock really, was the life of Chopin. I will never forget it – it opened up a world of creativity, sophistication, pain. And the wonderful music. When blood spots appeared on the keys as he played at the end I cried, and went home and cried some more.

Once, in Mervin, our parents, Auntie Eva and Uncle Askan, their boys Jimmie and Hughie, and Betty and I drove all the way to North Battleford to see a movie, *Snow White and the Seven Dwarfs*. We all got bubble gum to chew during the show. Jimmie was sitting behind me and kept leaning over my shoulder, I could hear him chewing in my ear.

After the movie Mom looked at me and said, What's in your hair? I don't know. It was bubble gum chewed into my hair, quite a lot of it, gum and hair. My mother was not happy, I had to get a very short haircut, which was okay by me, ringlets were a pain. I didn't miss the boring process involved in making ringlets in poker-straight hair. Short was cool and felt so nice in the wind.

In my teens and in Turtleford for something, I went to see *Gone With the Wind*. That opened my eyes. History. Love story. War. Clark Gable, the rat. Wow. Roy Rogers and Keemo Sabe were going to be boring now.

But it didn't matter what played. Friday night was show night in Livelong and everybody went.

First Drink

Dante Ferrari, alias Daddy of the salt-and-flour map, was a year or so ahead of me at school. The large Italian Ferrari family farmed close to Livelong, and for some inexplicable reason Dante invited me to Sunday supper when I was fourteen or fifteen. In a fit of anxiety, I worried incessantly about the upcoming event. The Ferraris were Catholic and I was afraid of committing some horrible faux pas. My dad's advice – Just do as the Romans do – was not helpful.

It was worse than I imagined. Mrs. Ferrari tried to make me feel comfortable and I relaxed until we were sat down to supper and for some reason I was seated across the large table from the parish priest. I was struck dumb. Struck envious, too, of the ten or eleven people around the table since I always wished we had a big family. With the Ferraris so numerous and talented and living out of town, Christmas concerts and talent nights couldn't begin until the back door opened and they filed in, the youngest to the oldest.

At each place that Sunday was a glass of wine Mister Ferrari had made himself. I had never even tasted anything alcoholic, was, in fact, dead set against it. I would never drink or smoke, in fact was seriously thinking about becoming a missionary or nun, but how could I be rude and not at least sip it? Which I did, sip, sip, sip to get rid of it and there was Mister Ferrari refilling my glass.

How many are there in your family? asked the priest. Oh, God, he was looking at me. It felt like a test.

Um four, I said. Well there were, counting my parents. He was not to be put off.

Four children? He looked like that was pretty poor, but maybe we weren't finished reproducing so there might be some hope for us.

I hung my head. Two.

Oh, the shame of it, how could my parents have failed me so miserably?

In my nervousness, I had almost finished the second glass of wine. I tried to smile at the priest, who had lost interest in me, and looked back at my plate, where a strange phenomenon had occurred.

The peas had disappeared off my plate and hovered nearby. After a quick check around the table to see if anyone had noticed, they appeared back on my plate. It kept it up, not just the peas, the whole plate was awfully, awfully far away, making it really, really difficult to eat, especially trying to stab the demonic peas.

Mercifully supper ended. I think Mrs. Ferrari wondered why so much of her delicious supper was still on my plate, and I couldn't think of how to explain it to her.

After supper Dante showed me around the farm. I loved all animals, so I liked the cow, a Jersey. Dante demonstrated how to milk her and asked if I'd like to try. I sat on the stool and leaned my face on the cow's side, I was awfully, awfully tired, and the cow was so nice and warm and motherly, so lovely, really, until I slid off the stool. I must have dozed off. The cow looked around at me, her big brown eyes sympathetic.

Sitting there on the ground, a warm feeling stole over me. I loved that cow. I loved the farm, I loved all the Ferraris, I even loved the priest - a strange syndrome that would surface every time I had too much to drink.

On the way home, Dante stopped the car and I threw up.

City Girl

It was exciting, my first trip to the big city of Saskatoon, bigger even than North Battleford, where we went to buy shoes at the store where the handsome Johnny Esaw waited on us. And where I ran to stick my foot in the x-ray machine that was supposed to help them pick your perfect size. You could watch your toe bones wriggling inside your foot.

Mom had an appointment at the Saskatoon Balsan Clinic. I recall it as some problem with her nerves, although my mother wasn't prone to nerve problems, or I didn't think so.

In the city I saw the Roxy Theatre with the name of the movie and the matinee time on the marquee and Dad said I could go.

I was fifteen, and wearing my cool blue cardigan with the white stripe on the sleeve, blue jeans and saddle shoes. I didn't think anyone would guess I wasn't a city girl. Or that this was my first time in an actual city theatre.

I bought my ticket and went in.

Pitch black. I could not see a thing. Feeling my way blindly down the aisle with my hand on the backs of the seats, after several rows I slid into a seat.

Something soft moved under me. I was sitting on a man.

I froze. Horrified. What to do? Leaping up screaming didn't seem polite, while the weird thought that I might hurt his feelings if I moved crossed my addled brain for a few split seconds before I gripped the seat in front, slowly rose and moved on shaking legs down the aisle to the other end of the row.

Once my eyes adjusted and I got up the nerve to look over at the large man, he was looking straight ahead as if nothing had happened. Maybe he thought he'd imagined it.

We were the only two people in the theatre.

I can't remember the movie.

Livelong Saturday Night

Saturday night Livelong was buzzing. Cars lining the streets, the stores open, hotel beer parlour doing a brisk business, pool room crowded with players and passersby checking out who was getting a haircut in Jimmy White's barber chair by the window. Clusters of people visiting on the boardwalks as the Ernie Summers band played a few come-on notes in the town hall. People streaming into town from all around the country. It was dance night.

I wasn't in any hurry to start going to the dances, despite Mom's and Betty's urging. On some level I suspected, as some religions do, that a whole lot of trouble lay in that direction. Like drinking and smoking, which I would have sworn on a stack of bibles never to do. My mother was mean enough to bring that up when I later embraced both with such enthusiasm.

I took to it like a duck to water. Who could resist the music of the Ernie Summers orchestra, we called it, though it was really a band, led by Ernie Summers's amazing saxophone. My friend Irene Brooks played the piano, alternating with my sister, Betty.

Ernie and his wife, Lillian, ran a grocery-and-what-not store where kids congregated in front of the comic book rack by the window. The whatnots included paintings by a woman north of Turtle Lake. She was also known for having many beautiful daughters with names like Emerald, Opal and so on. Once someone brought a shrunken human head, and that was a sensation.

Everyone came, if not to dance, then for the music and to sit on the benches that lined the wall and watch the dancing. Parents could keep an eye on their daughters and how often their sons went out for a nip from a bottle, but they came for the dancing too, and the older people were often the best dancers. An old bachelor, Martin Barlson, would often ask me for an old-time waltz, and he was the most amazing dancer. You seemed to float around, anchored by Martin's generous stomach. And I remember a couple, the O'Hares, who could cover more dance floor in one step than other people could in three, and every time they flew by we'd giggle and say Look, look, up in the air, It's a bird, it's a plane, it's Mrs. O'Hare! One of my poetic creations, I modestly admit.

Jean Simmons was there, clutching her little white dog against her chest, a brown home-rollie hanging from her bottom lip, ashes mingling with dog hair on her old maroon sweater. A lot of people smoked, a couple of brothers even smoked while dancing.

A man who lived out of town and who was either a bit simple of just painfully shy would cross the floor to where the girls waited and some of them hid in the cloakroom. I didn't mind dancing with him but wasn't above imitating him to the girls after – Gee, Loey, you sure are a swell dancer. He said it every time with great enthusiasm. We girls eyed the stag line without appearing to. Sometimes excitement was caused by the presence of the handsome RCMP officer from Glaslyn, or some other strangers arrived from one of the neighbouring towns. The word 'stag" in stag line made the dance sound like a mating season ritual. Well, in a way it was.

Square dances were positively dangerous, since the aim of some of the men was to swing the women off their feet. You wouldn't walk past a square dance if you valued your life.

Occasionally the back door crashed open and a couple of men trying to kill each other with their fists fell in. If the fight got too close, the women would scream and jump up on the benches. It was exciting.

At midnight the supper waltz was played and was often a sign of a serious relationship blooming since couples ate lunch together. Romance was always in the air. The women of the town supplied sandwiches and coffee.

Sometimes there were Box Socials, where women and girls would decorate a boxed lunch, hoping to attract the right bidder. Men would gather close to the stage, a beautifully done box was held up and they would make their bid, rivals pushing the price quite high with much shouting and egging-on from the crowd. Lunch with the owner went to the highest bidder.

I can see them all now. Feel the excitement. Hear the music.

Saturday nights have never been the same.

Blind Drunk

My parents were away. It was winter and four teen-agers sat on the floor around the heater in our small front room, getting drunk: Jimmy, my first love, so handsome I couldn't stop looking at him; Wally, a dear teddy bear of a guy and my first crush; Joyce Lofts, Wally's girlfriend and my best friend, who was staying with me.

Joyce and I had met at church camp at Turtle Lake. The four of us had become inseparable. I also stayed at the Lofts' house in Glaslyn, two towns away, where Mister Lofts, a big man, ran Lofts Garage. I was en-vious of their big, boisterous family. Joyce had three sisters, Helen, Elsie, and Myrtle, and an older brother, Bill, a tall, lanky guy who was usually folded up play-ing the saxophone on their large verandah. Upstairs in the girls' rooms at night you could hear Mister Lofts snoring from the downstairs bedroom. I think the house shook.

We sat around the heater that cold night, just talking

and laughing – we laughed a lot when we were together. We were innocents, good kids, none of us had had sex yet though the boys were seventeen. Joyce was fifteen, a year younger than I was, tall, slim and blonde with glasses. She had had polio and walked with an almost imperceptible limp. The four of us tore around the country in Wally's old brown Whippet, or Jimmy's model T that burned our feet, and when it got unbearable Jim stopped the car, took up some of the floorboards and poured in a gallon of water kept in the back for the purpose, and on we would go.

We were drinking beer, but suddenly I thought of my dad's bottle of Christmas brandy in the top kitchen cupboard. We each tried it and weren't keen but we had a couple of small drinks. Joyce, who hardly drank, had one. The combination of the heater, beer and brandy sent me into giggling fits until I heard a scream.

Joyce was up lurching around with her hands over her eyes. I'm blind! I'm blind!!

We all laughed.

Blind drunk? we all said, like we were playing charades.

Joyce was crying, *No! I can't see anything!*

Suddenly we were all scared spitless. Wally got up to hold her arm.

I can't see anything. Tears pouring down her face.

Oh God, it was for real. Joyce had gone blind and it must have been the brandy, it was my fault. Were we all going to go blind now? Oh, God, what to do in a little town with no doctor or hospital, no adult to take charge.

Wally decided. We'll go to Johnny and Irene's, he said. Johnny and Irene Swain, who ran the café were good to all the young people in town, almost like extra parents, and special friends of Wally's.

They won't be open, I said.

To their place in the back. The back of the café, he meant. That's where they lived when they weren't rushing around in the café. It was always busy. The only café in town. We all met there after school, drinking enough coke to eat our stomachs out.

Joyce was sobbing, feeling around like a blind person. Jim caught her hand as she reached toward the heater.

I wasn't sure that going to Johnny and Irene's was a good idea but we needed to do something. Before we all went blind, popped into my head. Going to parents was not even considered.

We went out of the house from the side door, out past the back gate and down the alley, Wally and Jim both helping Joyce, and me, full of guilt and worry, stumbling along behind. Poor Joyce, I didn't know what to say to her, it was just too awful. We'd all gone silent, negotiating the rutted, icy path, black with snowy patches. It was dead quiet, not even a dog barking, it must have been close to midnight. There was a moon.

Wally knocked, loud, two or three times on the door before Johnny, in his pyjamas, opened the door, Irene, in her bathrobe, not far behind.

Johnny didn't ask, just opened the door wide to let us all in and told us to sit down. He knew it was serious. I think we must have all tried to talk at once because I remember him saying, Settle down, now. Wally filled in the details, where we were, what we were doing, where my folks were.

My dad's brandy, I said. Guilty. Guilty. Guilty.

Irene put on a pot of coffee. Joyce huddled, sobbing, but quieter, almost as if she was afraid to bother them.

Johnny said Joyce was going to drink a couple of cups of coffee and we should all do the same, and we'd let a little time pass to see if Joyce regained her sight. He thought she would. He didn't elaborate.

But he'd given us hope. Even Joyce nodded, her eyes closed. Joyce and I both hated coffee. Wally sat with his arm around her, holding her hand. Her hand shook so he had to help her drink the coffee. Those two would go on to marry.

We emptied the pot and Irene put on more. After the second cup Joyce's sight started to come back. Half a cup more and it was back to normal. The smile on her face was beautiful.

What could have happened, we wondered.

Joyce was blind drunk, Johnny said. It wasn't just an expression. He'd heard of it, and thought that might be what it was.

Blind drunk. Joyce. Not Jimmy, or Wally, who drank more than they should, or me, who drank more than

With friends Maria Graham and Josie Farrari, Livelong, 1949.

I should. But Joyce, who rarely drank more than one beer – and that only to be sociable – who put up with her friends – who did.

Four chastened kids thanked Johnny and Irene from the bottom of their hearts. I can see them standing there in their nightclothes, smiling as they said goodnight, and the boys walked Joyce and me back home. There was no celebration, we'd all been too scared.

So scared surely none of us would touch alcohol ever again.

As if.

Sammy's Café

The summer after grade twelve, I got a job as a waitress at Sammy's café. The job would have been fine, enjoyable even, except for one thing. When the beer parlor in the hotel across the street opened at eleven, Sammy disappeared. Sammy was a short, dark-haired, charming man, perfect for the job, but Sammy was a drunk.

Sammy would tell me what the noon dinner was going to be, and he sounded like he was looking forward to making it. Before noon I'd wait on a farmer or two in town for supplies, one of the Tollefson brothers from the grocery store, Dick Mason from the garage, his kind eyes enormous behind coke bottle glasses, or maybe the handsome Rock Caplette would drop in for coffee before noon. I enjoyed waiting on them, they seldom wanted more than coffee, or a piece of toast. That I could handle, but I didn't have a clue about cooking, I'd never done any.

Mom was a wonderful cook. People would come to

the food booth at the Livelong Fair day and specifically ask for Mrs. Binns's apple or flapper pies. And I'd sit in school thinking about what we were having for dinner.

I'm just going out for a few minutes, Sammy would say when eleven o'clock rolled around. I didn't have the nerve to say I can't cook and that's not what you hired me for and I'm going to leave if you don't come back in time to make dinner. People took pity on my stumbling efforts but nobody went to the hotel and tapped Sammy on the shoulder. Or maybe they did and it didn't work.

I'd go by the elevator after work and moan about it and Dad would say oh just ask them if they'd like bacon and eggs or a sandwich, it's all right, they know it's not your fault. He never suggested quitting the job.

And then came the day of the picnic.

Betty had married Bill Graham and that summer we had a two-family picnic at Turtle Lake; my parents, Bill's parents, my grandma who lived with us, and my boyfriend Jim, and the rest of their family, including my friend Marina and Barry the blond brat who took great delight in chasing me with snakes or lizards. He would become a well-known architect in Calgary. Also two old Graham uncles who were visiting from Ontario. It was a beautiful day, lots of other families picnicking, swimming and going out in small rented boats.

After the picnic, the campfire had to be put out. Bill had that job and he and I were looking down at the faint embers, ready to smother them with sand. Most everyone else was up at the parking lot packing for the trip home. My grandma, tired from the day, was already in the car.

The old uncles, cleaning up the campground – an unnecessary exercise as trash was a rare sight – had found two large paint cans with lids, and for some odd reason put them on the dying embers.

Bill was to my right and slightly behind me when they exploded. The noise and the force of the burning paint threw me back onto the ground. I had no idea what had happened but when I saw the horrified faces looking down at me I knew it was bad. My face was black, crackling skin, my bangs, eyelashes and eyebrows burned off, the bits of skin not blackened flaming red. Jim took one look and ran for the car.

I was in his car with my parents in the back seat, Jim driving dangerously fast. Slow down, Jim, my dad said, there's no use killing us all. That struck me as funny when I remembered it later.

In Turtleford, Doctor Yaeger, the doctor who had ridden the railroad jigger from Turtleford to Mervin that cold winter night I got rheumatic fever, met us at the hospital. With forceps he carefully lifted the black crackling skin from my face while my parents and Jim stood and watched, their faces so serious I closed my eyes. The doctor must have given me something for the pain because I really didn't feel much. Third degree burns, he said.

That was the beginning of a long hospital stay, almost a month. The first morning in the hospital my dad came to see me. Mom didn't, she had a thing about hospitals.

Well, I have some good news and some bad news, Dad said, long before the good news/ bad news jokes came along. Oh my God, bad news, about scars I thought, or worse. Tell me the bad news first.

The bad news, he said, is that Bill is in the next room. He has second and third degree burns on his neck and arm. You were so bad that it was a while before they noticed his burns.

Oh, no. What's the good news, I asked.

Sammy burned down the café, he said.

Poor Sammy put a pot of oil on the stove and just nipped across the street for his morning pickup, either forgetting the pot, or forgetting I wasn't there.

I became Exhibit A at the hospital, my face swelling up like a cantaloupe about a week after admission. People stopped to stare in the door, and I was worried about what I was going to look like with no eyebrows or eyelashes, scars, and navy-blue blackheads driven into the pores in my nose. But the swelling gradually subsided, people found something else to look at, and I was discharged. The blueheads disappeared with scrubbing, and, amazingly, there were no permanent scars. I think Doctor Yaeger was a very good doctor.

Bill was only in hospital for a couple of days.

Of course my father didn't really mean the demise of Sammy's Café was good news, he was just trying to cheer me up. Sammy left town soon after. I hoped that, if he opened another café, it would not be across the street from a beer parlour.

Hitchhiking

I left Livelong to go to the Success Business College in Saskatoon when I was eighteen. It seems a strange choice now, numbers were not my strong suit, but Dad wanted me to have some job skills, and I liked what I'd seen of Saskatoon. Leaving that small town for the city was more difficult than I'd imagined. I knew no one, didn't know how to catch a streetcar, how to use a phone that wasn't bolted to the wall with people you knew talking – sometimes about you – when you lifted the receiver. I felt like the hick that I was.

At the YWCA I copied down a room-and-board address and someone kindly helped me find my way there. The landlady showed me the room, it was very small, and for some reason I didn't like the woman much, but handed over the rent money and went back to the YWCA to worry about the mistake I'd made. The story of my life.

However, this story would have a happy ending. Sitting in the lounge I saw a small, lively woman go to the desk and ask if there might be a girl from out of town who was looking for a boarding house. Her name was Mrs. Ennis.

I am, I said, getting up and going over to the desk. I knew the moment I saw her I wanted to live at her house. But what could I do about the money?

Mrs. Ennis sat down with me and I told her what I'd done and that I didn't want to live at that other place. She said, I would like you to live with us, too. You must go back and ask her for your money back. It won't be easy but you can do it. I really hope it will go well. And she gave me her phone number.

I got back on the streetcar and it was around four o'clock when I got back to that house. What do you want? she said. You aren't moving in until tomorrow.

When I told her I needed the rent money back she said a very firm No. Absolutely not. You rented the room. I could have rented to somebody else and you can't have the money back.

I didn't know what to do so I sat down in the living room. She asked what I was doing and I said I couldn't go without the money. Well, you will have a long wait, she said.

She went about her business and I sat there. Every once in a while she looked in and said Are you still here? You might as well go. You are not getting that money back and you have a lot of nerve to ask.

Boarders started appearing for supper, three of them, all men. Not another girl who could be my friend. I could see them in the dining room and they could see me. They kept looking over, no doubt wondering what I was doing there. I'm still hungry, one of the guys said when they left the table. Me, too, another one said. I could hear dishes being washed and put away. It was starting to get dark out.

Finally the woman came back into the room. Are

you going to keep sitting there? she said and I said yes. I was almost in tears.

I could hear her talking about me with someone. I don't know what to do with her, she said.

About ten minutes later she came back in and gave me the money. Not too graciously, but what matters graciousness when you're desperate? And maybe I didn't deserve it. Thank you, I said.

Just go, she said. Just go.

On the bus I counted it. It was all there.

And that's how I came to live with the Ennises.

I loved the Ennises. Meals were congenial. Mister Ennis and I did the dishes every night. He was a sweet, gentle man. He washed and I dried, and we made the same joke every time about the Joy dishwashing liquid. He taught me a flashy way to shuffle cards. I especially came to love Mrs. Ennis and am sorry to say I lost touch with them. Life takes different turns and it seems someone is always left behind.

I was thinking about their house on 9th Street when I wrote the Sgt. Wilson story and poor Polly Wilson's lonely wait in a two storey house on 9th Street in Saskatoon for them to get a place so she could send for the children, whom she would never see again.

Mrs. Ennis was a wonderful cook, and I had a roommate, Phyllis, in her twenties, I guessed, who had a job. We shared the double bed and got along well. I can see the handsome man who lived there but can't remember his name. Les Ennis, a son, lived in a third floor room, and had all kinds of gadgets he'd made, for turning out the light when he was in bed and other conveniences.

I enjoyed the school, made friends and was having fun. Going to dances with nice guys in a wonderful blue dress. Writing silly poems about the principal,

Mister Furse. It's amazing how words rhyme with Furse. Getting to know the city. In "Falling In Love With Words," I tell about my not distinguishing myself at Success Business College. I knew office work wouldn't figure largely in my future and I felt guilty for the money it cost Dad and Mom to send me.

But it was something I could do – sort of – if necessary. And I could type like the wind. I even had typewritten dreams, reading from the pages what was happening. Someone else told me she had the same weird experience.

I had been living with the Ennises for five or six weeks when I felt homesick and decided to hitchhike home. Eighteen years old and stupid. I acted on impulse, which has got me into trouble too many times.

I wasn't on the highway long before an enormous truck, maybe what they call an eighteen wheeler though I didn't count, pulled over. Way above me a very big arm pushed the passenger door open and a very big guy leaned over.

Whereya going?

The road that goes through North Battleford and north, I called back, to Livelong.

Hop in.

More like climb in. Several steps up.

I should wait for a family, I thought, starting up the steps, this guy is scarily huge. I got in and he reached over and shut the door. I wondered if it was hard to open if you had to get out in a hurry. He was heading for Meadow Lake.

I can take you as far as Glaslyn, he said. And we were off. His name was Gary.

Gary liked to sing "I'm a little spruce bug, happy as can be" and I relaxed immediately. I couldn't imagine a serial killer singing "I'm a Little Spruce Bug" as he sawed me into little pieces, but who knows?

Like to read? he asked after awhile. There's some magazines in the glove compartment.

Someday I'll get married, sang Gary as I checked out the magazines, have a home up in a tree...

True Romance, True Story, Modern Romance et cetera. No books featuring tied-up women screaming on the covers. I'd lucked into the gentle giant. A romantic gentle giant.

I read a short piece, to please him mostly, but the view from up there was so amazing I put it down. It was a bit like flying low over the countryside. In a crop duster, maybe, without the smell. I relaxed and started to enjoy the adventure. Gary had a girlfriend, he told me, and was hoping to get married soon. That explained a lot.

Most fields were harvested, the odd one still in gleaming gold swaths; black summerfallow, dazzling yellow trees, great splashes of red, orange, wine, with the odd dark spruce beginning to mingle as we headed north. All this and the western sun warm on haystacks, farm buildings, horses. Someday I'll get married, sang Gary, build a home up in a tree, as the miles went by.

Too soon, we were in Glaslyn and Gary asked if I wanted to call home but I didn't want to tell the folks I was hitchhiking. In the blink of an eye, we were through Glaslyn. Be careful who you take a ride with, Gary said, as we neared my stop. And at the junction to Highway 22 to Livelong I said goodbye to Gary, the romantic truck driver. It's strange how you can feel so fond of someone you've just met. I hoped a really nice girl would marry Gary, if she didn't mind living in a tree.

Dusk wasn't far off, and I started to wish I had called from Glaslyn, Dad would have come and got me. He'd be upset but was going to be anyway when I got home. In grade nine my friend Marlys and I hitchhiked to North Battleford and Dad had to come and drive me home. I don't know why Marlys wasn't there on the drive back but she wasn't. He was very quiet on that trip and I knew how much I'd disappointed him.

I'd just decided to go back to Glaslyn and call home when an old rattling farm truck started slowing down. A farmer, older than my father. No worries there. I got in.

He was a small, wiry man. He hardly said a word, and wasn't likely to break into song either, so we bumped along, large rolls of wire shifting and rustling in the truck box. I thought about Gary, singing his way to Meadow Lake. Someday I would like to marry someone like Gary.

Not far from Fairholm, the little town before Livelong, the driver slowed as we drew abreast of a fence on the left. From a wide leaning gate a faint trail rose on an incline through a large empty clearing. Gotta take this wire up there, he said. 'Up there' was a house giving in to gravity, and not much else that I could see. Maybe it was where he kept his farm equipment, I thought, trying to ignore a little *frisson* of fear.

We turned in and rattled along the trail, pulling up to the house and then around it as he muttered something about a shed. I couldn't see a shed, and moved closer to the door.

He killed the motor, reached across and yanked me over. Oh, Jesus, rape. I struggled hard, punching him, biting his arm, kicking his legs, and raking a heel down his shin. He let go. I grabbed the door handle and pitched out onto the ground. He raced around the truck and as I scrabbled up, he jerked me close. I struggled and struggled but he was strong, much,

much stronger than he looked. As we fought I saw an abandoned stone well half hidden in the brush and something said, If you don't get away you'll end up there. Terror drove my knee into his crotch, and I bolted, his outraged howl behind me.

Running past the house and down the clearing, with the picture of that well in my head, my feet almost didn't touch the ground. I risked a glance back, he wasn't there, thank God, but I didn't slow down.

And then I heard the truck starting, squealing around and coming fast. Oh God he was chasing me with his truck. I zigzagged in wide arcs and he had to slow down on the turns but kept coming. Closer now. He was trying to kill me. I saw him as he turned, hunched down, eyes glaring, he was going to run me down with his truck so I wouldn't tell. I ran and ran and on he came.

Close to the fence he had to swerve and drive away from me to turn around. Don't let him see me, I prayed, squeezing under the barbed wire and diving into a bush across the road. A thick bush, thank God, and I didn't dare try to see the truck, but it was coming.

I lay on my stomach, it was almost dark now. Just lay there scarcely breathing, as he drove slowly, very, very slowly back and forth, back and forth, over and over, rattle, rattle, rattle, wire rolls rustling, trying to see me. My heart lurched into my throat, I crawled on my belly a little farther where the bushes were thicker and higher. Some small soft thing nudged my hand. I ignored it, afraid to move a muscle. I touched a pain on my head, sticky with blood. My torn, bloody jacket.

I would stay here all night if I had to. But finally, revving the motor so loud it felt like a message, he kept going. I lay there and shook so hard it must have rustled the bushes but it was finally completely dark before I had the courage to leave, crawling out of the bushes and out of the ditch into the lights of a car I hadn't seen coming. Before I could think what to do, it stopped. A light came on in the car and the driver got out.

Are you hurt? he asked and I saw the anxious face of his wife, and two little boys in the back. I burst into tears. He helped me into the front seat beside his wife. I couldn't stop crying. He started the car and she took my cold hands in her two warm ones and said, It's all right. It's all right. You're safe, which made me cry harder.

When I calmed down the man asked me what had happened, and I said I hitch-hiked and got in the wrong car. Truck. But I'd got away and he hadn't hurt me. I was all right, just scared. He wondered if we should call the police but I was so terrified of the man I was afraid to.

They were going to Turtleford but went out of their way and drove me home. Such wonderful people.

I never told my parents what really happened that night, and they never insisted. My wonderful suede fringed jacket was ruined, the head wound minor. It was a car accident, I lied.

I never forgot the terror of that experience, and have always wanted to write a novel about this happening to a woman the man would rape before she got away. The rotten guy she was engaged to used it as an excuse to dump her and her life went downhill, taken over by an all-consuming need for revenge. Which she must carry out on her own. The barbed-wire man would end up, á la Steven King, in the old stone well.

I must have seemed different when I got back to Saskatoon because I still have a letter Mrs. Ennis wrote to my mother to say she was worried, I was so quiet when I came back, and she thought something might have happened to me on that trip.

I never told anyone for years what had happened that day, but just telling it such a long time later made my heart race.

Saskatchewan Hospital

I had been interviewed, accepted, and Dad drove me to the Saskatchewan Hospital in North Battleford to report for work. I hadn't found a secretarial job and this appealed to me.

It was dusk when we arrived and he parked the car beside the nurses' residence. Large buildings loomed everywhere and in a lighted upstairs room a sad woman with extremely short hair was looking out a barred window. I didn't like the bars on the windows but what did I expect, the hospital at that time was for seriously mentally ill people. I thought it would be an interesting job.

It was that in spades.

A very short woman, the house mother, Jonesy, was expecting me. She took me to a room upstairs and introduced me to my roommate, Donna Dowd. She looked like a good sort. Donna introduced me to Ella Phelps, next door, and another, very cute, very chatty girl called Mac, short for MacMillan. We were all called by our last names on the wards, and it seemed to carry over to life after work. Phelps and Mac were on the night shift, Dowd on days, and would take me to work with her in the morning.

The wards were a bit of a shock at first – strange smells, raucous laughter, screams, arguments, crying, sometimes fighting – fortunately not all happening at once. The noise level depended on the ward.

I liked the head nurse who took me around introducing me to staff and patients. One of the patients was Ardith McRae, a quiet young woman I saw putting clean sheets on a bed. I wondered why she was there, but she was not the only patient on the wards to appear normal and do small jobs.

Ardith was tall, and very strong looking, with one eye looking in one direction, the other somewhere else, and poker-straight short black hair.

Queen Victoria, who never left her room, or her bed, was another. She was a staff favorite. A little bow or curtsy was expected when entering and leaving her room, the only single room I remember. She was a pretty little lady – woman, I almost said, but there was something ladylike about Queen Victoria. I curtsied and said, I'm honoured to meet Your Majesty. We had a little chat and I bowed when we left.

She was quite friendly for royalty, I said. You're going to fit right in here, Binns, said the head nurse. What did that mean? You're taking patients to a movie in the gymnasium at two o'clock, she said. You'll enjoy it, it's an easy job for your first day, Ardith will take you. Ardith was nodding and smiling.

Just me and the patients? I asked, feeling nervous but trying not to show it.

Just six quiet patients from here, some relaxing time for your first day. They love westerns so you won't have any trouble. I wished Ardith would stop smiling.

At two the patients lined up and we were given popcorn. And shortly we were in the gym, the patients excited, sitting with their friends. I sat on the chair in the aisle, Ardith next to me. Nurses were in other aisle chairs so I relaxed. And soon the movie started. What a fun job.

The movie started with cartoons and screams of laughter, I hoped no one would choke on the popcorn. I enjoyed the cartoons, too, they were good back then.

When the movie started things quieted down. I relaxed and felt good about how things were going my first day.

Until I felt something lightly stroking my bare arm. Arm hair up. Goosebumps everywhere. Did I imagine that?

No, there it was again. And a whisper in my ear, *I'm going to kill you.*

I looked at Ardith. She was smiling at me. *I'm going to kill you*, she said again, stroking my arm. Every hair on my body stood at attention. With the flickering light from the screen and her wild eyes, she looked downright terrifying.

Oh. God. Oh, God, what do I do? I couldn't run out screaming. Whatever made me think I wanted this job? I'm quitting after this movie.

She did it again. *I'm going to kill you.* Stop that, Ardith! I hissed, my heart hammering. Don't touch me.

She got interested in the movie and I calmed down, sort of. But about the time my heart slowed down to just twice as fast, it came again, the whisper I'm going to kill you. The stroking. The face looming eerily in the half-light. It was a horror movie.

Finally, the ordeal ended and we started back to the ward. I didn't even look at Ardith.

The head nurse and the other nurse were having coffee in the little kitchen. How was the movie? they said. Well, it was...can I talk to you? Sure, what's the problem. She didn't look as concerned as I thought she should.

I noticed Ardith drifting closer to listen. I couldn't really tell with her there, she'd kill me for sure, and I wanted to live long enough to escape.

Anything odd happen? Both nurses were smiling. Ardith, too, grinning from ear to ear, looking at me, I think, though it was hard to tell. Ardith was obviously trying not to laugh.

They all were.

Light dawned.

Oh, no. An initiation prank, and Ardith was in on it. They all laughed and laughed.

So where do I leave my letter of resignation? *You shits*, I wanted to add but didn't think I knew them well enough. You scared the bejeesus out of me. That made them laugh some more. It was just the funniest thing. Downright hilarious.

So Ardith isn't really going to kill me? More laughter.

No, but I sure scared you, Ardith said.

That she did.

On another ward, not much later, they also liked to scare the bejeesus out of new people. They sent me on the early morning walk through the long, empty concrete basement with the woman who picked up the breakfast for the ward. She had killed several people, her whole family, they made sure I knew. And knew that I had that job for a month.

She was a big woman with coal-black hair, large hands and the biggest, hairiest legs I'd ever seen. She never said a word on those silent mornings, the only sound the rattling of the cart on the concrete floor, and me babbling to her until it dawned on me that maybe I should shut up. I heard she'd only killed family members, but maybe because they talked too much. Haven't we all felt like it?

She never spoke, not to anyone, it was thought she'd had a shock. I suppose killing your entire family might qualify. A worse shock for them.

Some of the cases were so sad. There was Johnny, early twenties, who had not been accepted by her father because she was a girl, and had lived in the barn with the animals her whole life until someone reported it. Johnny moved very fast but on all fours, and made animal sounds, so real you'd think you were in the barn with them. Whinnies, mooos, barks, meows, clucking and more. I like to think the dogs and cats were her friends and kept her warm at night. Nothing was ever done to her father.

Gradually, Johnny learned a few words but not many, and her preferred way of getting around remained the way she came in with. But she started to laugh, which was a miracle. And to like some people, an even bigger one.

I was there two years and we all had to help with shock treatments. It was awful. Putting the thick cardboard wad in the patient's mouth, their eyes wide with fear, and holding the body down to prevent the violent jerking from breaking bones or throwing joints out of place. I know they are doing shock again in hospitals, a far cry, I know, from the way it was done then, but still. I never saw a patient get enough better to justify it, and often they were worse, catatonic almost, for a long time. I talked to someone recently who had worked on the grounds with patients, and he said he'd worked with two men who had amazing recoveries after the treatment.

We also watched a poor soul undergo a prefrontal lobotomy which didn't make me long to be a surgeon. The lobotomy patient, a woman, didn't get any better.

There was only one totally catatonic woman, who

never moved a muscle, day after day. Standing, not sitting down, and with one arm raised to the side.

3A was our violent ward, and in my second year a decision was made to take violent patients from the Weyburn Hospital in exchange for our physically ill patients – our dear Queen Victoria went – which didn't seem like a good trade. The new patients arrived in the afternoon, and we worked a double shift to accommodate them and – since of course they were anxious – to reduce the number of new people they had to adjust to.

One of the women from Weyburn had had her right arm amputated a few inches above the wrist. She was my charge and I tried to talk to her but she wouldn't speak. She looked very angry, her arms crossed, not looking at anyone. I took her a drink of juice, which she threw on the floor.

When it was time to get them ready for bed – the bathroom call first – she was not happy. The 3A women's bathroom door opened the wrong way. You had to push it open from the hall, and pull it open from inside. I'd heard nurses complaining it was dangerous. Tired from the double shift, I did a very stupid thing. I sat the patient on the toilet and I knelt in front of her to take off her shoes.

Wham! I hit the floor, clubbed in the head by her powerful stump and she was on me, grabbing for my throat as my head hit the cement floor. There were some patients in the bathroom, I remember Mrs. Penley, who could swallow a small orange whole, looking down at me with interest and scratching her crotch, as usual. I struggled but the woman was very strong and mad. Really, totally mad. She let go of my throat to hit me on the head and I yelled Get the nurse! at Mrs. Penley, who smiled but didn't stop scratching. Get the nurse! between punches – Mrs Penley laughing now as I finally twisted around to where I could kick the hall wall. The door flew open and two nurses pulled the woman off, not without a struggle. Bruises, a black eye, red neck and sore throat and a huge lump on my head should call for a day off, I thought, but no one else did. Never mind, I was alive.

The door was replaced not long after that.

Another patient I remember. An enormous woman named Joy, whom they called the idiot. That was her diagnosis. The only thing that seemed to help her was a tub bath. Joy weighed 400 pounds. It took at least three of us to get her in and out of the tub, all drenched.

I made good friends there. My roomate, Dowd, was great fun. When we were both on days we set the radio alarm and when it came on with "God Save the Queen" we stood at attention while lying stiff in bed. We laughed every time. *The Harry Dekker Show* came on after that. Much later, he would be my boss at CJNB radio station, the best job ever.

My other close friend, Ella Phelps, became a friend for life. One day on the ward the head nurse asked El and me to bathe an old woman who had died. Her family was coming to pick up her body. We looked at each other, we didn't want to do it but of course had to. And we treated that old woman with the utmost respect, bathing her, combing her hair, putting on a fresh gown and saying a prayer when we finished for her and her family. She looked very nice.

People who worked at the hospital were a young, party-loving crowd. And we never missed a chance to party. Quite heavy drinking was the norm, not on the hospital grounds, which were beautiful, and still are, just above the North Saskatchewan River and the bridge to what they call the Old Town, Battleford, as opposed to North Battleford. The riverbank was the site of lots of parties, one that ended in a mud fight.

Young people on our own, we drank too much, a lot of us. A few of us would gather on the beds in the women's residence and trade stories of the wards over a beer. We laughed so much our stomachs hurt, sometimes falling off the bed, and laughed some more.

On one afternoon shift on a quiet ward in 1953 I watched the crowning of Queen Elizabeth on a small cloudy TV. I was transfixed by that young, pretty woman, the solemnity of it, and the crown that looked much too heavy on her head.

It was a great job but I didn't want to make a career of it. After two years it was time to go. I'm glad to have had the unique experience of working there. A lot of friends were getting married but I just wasn't ready to settle down. I was confused and, I realized later, depressed.

About this time my folks moved to Turtleford, the next town to Mervin, and I got a job there working for the local lawyer, a very kind, courtly old gentleman, while I tried to sort myself out. My mother kept a letter he wrote her after I left. He said I had a pleasant personality and was good in dealing with his clients. He also said I was efficient. He never saw me trying to decipher my mangled shorthand scribble. I'm glad he wrote that letter so my parents would know my stint at Success Business College hadn't been a total waste.

I should have taken his letter along when I went to Calgary to look for a job. But that experience probably got me my next job.

Calgary

Brazil

Calgary Years
My Skirt
Unforgivable

Getting There
Señor Cotta
The Buzzard
Hurricane Hazel

Calgary Years

I can't remember why I chose Calgary instead of, say, Saskatoon, which I liked very much and where I actually knew people. It's as much a mystery to me now as it was then, as if I picked the name out of a hat. I should have left it there.

I got a job at California Standard Oil, where a feeling of energy and excitement was in the air. New oil wells coming in. New discoveries. My little corner of California Standard, in an office with a great woman boss, was good. I was a file clerk on a file clerk's salary, but I was just happy not to have a job where taking shorthand and keeping books was expected. My job was filing drilling logs, long, thin, unintelligible pieces of paper. The filing cabinet had long narrow drawers, and I had to stand on a low platform to file them.

One funny incident was a woman running around with a teletype message, Jesús is coming, it said. Jesús was a Mexican engineer, the first time I heard it as a name except in church.

I liked the people who worked there and made friends. I went skating several times with the funniest guy I ever met; I thought how much fun it would be for whoever he married.

Humour is underestimated in many situations and relationships. I find funny people irresistible. In the books I devoured at that time, it was almost nonexistent. As if you couldn't have a serious theme that included humour. I especially treasured the books that made me laugh.

I read for enjoyment then, and still do, about other countries, other occupations. I especially love spy stories set in Russia and Germany, and fiction and nonfiction about the Second World War. I love reading about super-smart people. I always knew good writing from bad, but I began to read more classics, more good women writers, more nonfiction. Becoming a writer was in the back of my mind, and I attached stories to people I saw – on the bus, in restaurants, on the street. Once, in a small coffee shop, I was close to a table with two women who had a lot to talk about. I am an incorrigible eavesdropper. They were talking about a friend with marriage problems, and then one said, And you know what he wanted her to do? I leaned closer. But the awful thing was whispered mouth to ear. My guess was a threesome, or maybe he wanted her to poison his boss who was coming to dinner. Or maybe he just wanted her to go on a diet.

My social life was enjoyable, going to Banff and learning to ski with a nice guy, just a friend, and another couple. The other woman was called Rosemary, a model-pretty blonde who was an amazing skier. She shared a room with the guy, which was still unusual in the '50s, and she rarely said anything to me directly. I was a novice skier and maybe she couldn't be bothered.

And going to parties, of course and there were a lot of nice guys there. I lived in a boarding house where the landlady was not the kind, friendly type, not wonderful Mrs. Ennis. She disapproved of young women going out at night, disapproved of them period. Doreen, the other boarder, became a friend. The table was always laid just so, the offering of the day under a silver cover, but we often got up from the table hungry. I suspected the landlady of snooping through my things, looking for proof that I was up to something.

And then the proof arrived. A few days after spending the day at the Calgary Stampede, a letter arrived for me from the Calgary Police Department. She was holding it when I arrived home from work. Here's a letter for you, she said. *I knew it all along.* Waiting for me to open it.

Mystified and nervous, I took the letter into my room and shut the door. I need to know what it's about, she called through the door. You are living in my house. The letter was to inform me that my keys, which I had lost at the Stampede, had been turned in and I could come pick them up at the police station. I walked out and handed her the letter.

It was a habit of mine at that time to stop in at Catholic churches, to relax and to say a prayer or two, but mostly just to take in the atmosphere. I loved it all, the flickering candles, the statues, the kneeling, and was thinking of becoming a Catholic. I even had a rosary.

My French sort-of boyfriend was delighted. He asked me to go with him to an evening service. I was just ahead of him going in and was going to genuflect before sitting when I sprawled in the aisle. He'd thought I was going to shame him by not genuflecting, and pushed me down from behind. My ardour cooled very quickly. For Catholicism. And for him.

I never did learn the entire rosary, but still have moments of envying nuns. Maybe we all do. Such a simple life it looks from the outside. But I still liked stopping at Catholic churches, and Anglican churches. Since joining the Anglican church after church camp summers, I went to church wherever I was. Anglican, Lutheran, United, whatever was handy – sometimes just to think where it was quiet. About what to do with my life, which didn't have much meaning, wasn't going anywhere. I did want to marry and have children. It's sad that churches can't be open now, for people to think in.

Being a missionary was no longer in my future. Had not been since I'd started going to the Livelong dances and thought of all the fun I'd be missing in some far-flung country. It made me feel lonely just thinking about it.

People were friendly at work, and my best friend in Calgary, a wonderfully funny girl, Anne Korkosh, also worked there. She lived with her four funny sisters. I liked them all and envied them their closeness. I was at their big apartment one night when an encyclopedia salesman came to the door. He had a doleful look, and they started asking him if he liked his job. He said he didn't. So why was he doing it if he didn't like it, and just think of all the interesting things he could be doing if he wasn't going door to door with those heavy books, he looked too smart for that, and by the tine he left he was going to quit that damned job, he had never liked it, and it was hard on his back, and he was going back to university. I don't know what he ended up doing but hope it was good.

Anne and her sisters left after my first year in Calgary. Two of them got jobs in Vancouver, and they wanted to stay together. I started to hang around with my house-mate, Doreen, and Gwen, who was from Saskatchewan. Her brother-in-law was my sister Betty's first serious boyfriend.

Gwen wanted to move, and we decided to get a place together. Doreen stayed on at the boarding house. I don't think we looked very long because we moved into a depressing place, an upstairs suite in a house, small windows. I must have fallen for the easy chair with a flowered slipcover, the only nice thing in that place. But even it wasn't comfortable.

Gwen turned out to be a very bossy roommate. She would call me at work and say it was my turn to clean the place, or do the laundry, or buy groceries, whatever, and to go home to do it right after work. I'll admit I was the messy one, but didn't really enjoy having a crabby mother for a roommate. But couldn't move again.

Well, I wasn't finished with that.

My Skirt

While still living at the boarding house in the summer, I got a call from California Standard's MIT golden boy, graduated at sixteen or something like that from the Massachusetts Institute of Technology – degrees and more degrees – who had been out in the field all summer. His name was David Rostoker. He called to ask me to go a movie, *The Student Prince*, when he got back in town. I only knew him to see him, and the thought of going out with him was daunting to say the least.

Getting ready the next day I put on my mustard-coloured knitted suit. Who in their right mind buys a mustard-coloured suit? Those suits were all the rage and were certainly comfortable, the skirt having an elasticized waistband, covered by the long top. They must have been out of other colours.

The doorbell rang and I answered. There stood a man with a very long, very bushy, very black beard. You hardly ever saw anyone with a beard back then. Hello, he said. Are we ready to go? I hardly recognized him.

We walked to the bus stop and caught the bus downtown. I wasn't the only person who found the beard interesting. I probably talked too much on the trip, a habit when not knowing what to say. He smiled, beautiful white teeth in all that foliage.

We had a fairly long walk from the bus to the theatre. I asked about his summer in the field and he said it was marvelous. He was very tanned and quite handsome, really, talking about his great summer.

The theatre, which was about half full, had a few empty seats about halfway down. They were green, of some plushy material, and the empty seats were the kind that flipped up when not in use, the front edge topmost. We sat down, David put his seat down first but I sat on the flipped-up part and slid into the seat.

It was my first time in the theatre and I glanced around a bit as he told me more about his exciting summer. I was beginning to feel comfortable. The movie would start soon with no need to think about what to say. I started to put my shoulder-bag purse on my lap.

I was wearing something white.

Stunned, I bent down, trying to make sense of what I was seeing.

I was wearing something white.

It must be a trick of light. I shut my eyes and looked again.

I was sitting in my slip.

Where was my skirt? How was this possible? Really. Did I forget to put it on? Walk to the bus, ride the bus in just my slip? Walk from the bus and all the way down Eighth Avenue without a skirt? I thought people were looking at his beard. Wouldn't he have noticed or was his brilliant mind preoccupied with brilliant engineer thoughts?

Where's my skirt? I hissed.

He looked shocked. And I saw the same thoughts going through his head. Was she not wearing a skirt when I picked her up? Did I ride on the bus and walk all that way downtown with a woman with no skirt? Maybe that's why people were looking at us.

Where's my skirt?

Shhhhh! I didn't take that kindly. He wasn't the one wearing half a suit.

Gritted teeth. Where is my bloody skirt? Like he should know.

I don't know.

Neither do I, I said, peering at the floor. It wasn't there. Where could it go? Didn't I have it on before?

 I thought you did.

I did, too. Starting to laugh. Hysteria. I lose clothes a lot, maybe I was a stripper in another life, but this was ridiculous.

Moving my feet out from under the chair, I felt something.

There it was, all bunched down around my ankles, my feet hidden by the seat the first time I looked.

He politely looked away as with difficulty and in the throes of a laughing fit I squirmed my way back into the skirt.

The plushy seat must have stripped it off, I said. It has an elastic waist.

Yes, I can see that it could. His engineer's mind at work.

He laughed. The movie started.

The beard was beginning to grow on me.

We went out occasionally but he told me at the start that he had someone back in Boston. He liked my company, he said. And he laughed every time he said it. I met her when she joined him in Calgary, she was very nice and looked like someone who probably kept her clothes on in public.

Unforgivable

Some things that happen in life hurt us, something said that cut to the bone perhaps, but we forgive and forget. As others forgive and forget our sins. But there is one that remains, when remembered, unforgivable.

This one is mine.

I had been working at California Standard Oil for two years. I liked the women I worked with. Gladys, the boss of our small area, was a great woman who had been a hairdresser for years. She once told us a story about her temperamental hairdresser boss, who was easily riled if someone complained about the job he was doing. One unfortunate man did complain and it was apparently the last straw for the boss, who took the electric clippers and shaved a strip right up and over the middle of his head, then threw down the clippers and walked out, never to return. Of course these days the poor guy could just shave his head but if it happened back then you had to hide till your hair grew out.

One weekend Doreen, Gwen and I caught an early bus to Banff for the day. None of us could afford to stay over and would catch a bus back. We rented skis and enjoyed the day. They took a beginner lesson and I skied because I had been to the mountains quite a few times. My turns were getting really smooth and I'd reached the stage where skiing was beginning to be wonderful.

In the lodge we were chatted up by some nice guys from the States who were real skiers. They invited us to their place for a drink and we thought nothing of it, just a pleasant way to pass the time before the bus. They were fun and there was safety in numbers.

They had a super nice cabin, and we had a couple of drinks and enjoyed their company and beautiful view from there. They ordered pizza. I'd been talking a lot to a guy called Dave, and suddenly noticed that Gwen and Doreen weren't there.

They must be in the bathroom, I thought, and checked. They were not in the bathroom. I went outside and called and called but they didn't answer. They had left without me. They had gone and left me there with three strange guys.

How could they? Why would they? I'll never forget that feeling, like your insides are falling.

I went back inside and asked for a ride to the bus depot, but the last bus was leaving and it was almost dark. I didn't know what to do, scared to leave the cabin since I really didn't know where it was and where would I go anyway. One of the guys brought out a pillow and a blanket and put them on the back of the couch.

After awhile they started to go to bed. I sat in the chair, trying not to cry. I think they were decent guys, but still, I didn't know them.

You're scared, aren't you? Dave said, and then I did cry.

Those girls did a terrible thing to you, he said. Are they supposed to be your friends?

They are, I said. Or they were.

Good, tell them to fuck off, he said, getting up to arrange the blanket and pillow on the couch. He was the first person I knew to say "fuck off". You can sleep and I'm going to sit here all night so you don't have to worry.

I did sleep, and in the morning Dave was still sitting in the chair. I was so grateful to that lovely young man. He drove me to the bus depot.

I sat on the bus trying to think of what to do, and not just about the very nasty, unforgivable thing Gwen and Doreen had done.

A few years ago I received a letter from Doreen, who'd met someone on a bus who told her where I lived. She was excited about renewing the friendship. I threw the letter away. Now you know what a small-minded person I am. And I'm sorry actually, she wasn't a bad person. She just went along with Gwen. But still.

And maybe that Banff trip was a wakeup call that my life was going in a direction I didn't want. I was falling for my boss, the one our office reported to, and had enough sense to know I didn't want to have an affair with a married man. He had children, too.

A huge change was in order, but I didn't know where to start. Give notice at work? Find another job? Move out and find another place? How and where to go, living from paycheck to paycheck. I didn't even tell my 'friends' what a cruel, malevolent thing they had done. Gwen called it a joke. I had to live with Gwen and stopped going out much. Depression settled in along with inaction.

Then along came Jack. A geological engineer who looked like Jack Palance, who said on about the fourth date, Do you want to get married and go to Brazil?

That was a thought.

Getting There

He hit me the first time the day after the wedding. We were going out for breakfast in Saskatoon when he saw my housecoat on a chair, and said, Hang that up. I will when we get back, I said, wanting to be somewhere I was not alone with him. Hang it up, he said again, and when I didn't do it fast enough – I didn't like being ordered to – he hit me. Punched my arm so hard I almost fell.

I hung it up.

Shocked and scared. My own fault. I knew before we married that it was a mistake, already a bit scared of him, but didn't have the guts to back out. Or to leave him after that first punch.

His sister Janet also had a mean streak. We had stopped to visit her and her husband before leaving. I'd slept late and she set the table for breakfast for me with every single item from her silverware wedding chest, and watched with a little smile while I tried to guess which spoon and fork to use for what. So classy.

The 'honeymoon' in New York was not something I like to remember. I wasn't hit but wondered when it would happen again. He didn't talk much, hardly at all, and it was worse than being alone in a big, strange city. Maybe he was sorry, too. He didn't seem any happier than I was.

I remember two things: the sight of New York from so high on the Statue of Liberty, how the walkway and the railing didn't feel safe. And seeing Marilyn Munroe.

Out for a walk one evening we saw a small crowd gathered around something on a corner. We walked over and had a close-up view of the making of the famous photo, Marilyn laughing in a cream-coloured dress with the skirt flying up. I think of that night every time I see that photograph on the wall of my favourite restaurant, the Broadway Café in Saskatoon.

Then we were on a freighter bound for Brazil. I don't know if we travelled that way for economy's sake or if it appealed to Jack as something of an adventure.

That it certainly was. There were very few other passengers. We, or maybe just I, talked a lot to a beautiful woman missionary. She and her sons and their pale, silent wives were going back to a mission up or down the Amazon River from our destination, Belem. I found the sons and wives creepy, but I liked her.

Having had at one time a sincere desire to become a missionary, maybe even a nun in my Catholic phase, I was interested in her mission. She told me a lot about their work there, and the actual dangers of the place, the trip there on a barge, where you didn't dare dangle your fingers over the side if you still liked them, since the swarms of piranha also liked fingers, and everything they attached to. She had once seen a native man squeezed to death by a boa constrictor, unable to save him. And she told me a story I never forgot.

One morning one of the little native boys came running to tell her something about a big snake, and something about frogs, down at the end of the garden. She ran down and saw an incredibly large snake lying there with its mouth wide open, and small frogs hopping from everywhere falling over each other to jump into its mouth. That snake had mesmerizing powers. Some of them do.

What seems like a lifetime later I told that story sitting next to Jack Hodgins in the dining room at the Saskatchewan Summer School of the Arts.

What an amazing metaphor, Jack said.

For what? I asked.

For war, he said. And of course it was.

I think the missionary suspected something amiss and invited me to go see her at the mission she told me about. I wish now I'd gone, finger-eating fish or not. They also had a mission in Belem for people who needed help, and she was there sometimes. I went after a couple of months but she wasn't there. The woman I tried to talk to seemed puzzled and kind of shocked. Well, what could she say, really? She probably only knew sensible people.

Our cabin on the freighter was tiny. A bunk on each side separated by about three feet of floor, and a shower so small you had to bend your head back to avoid it getting drenched every time, and made washing your hair impossible. Claustrophobic, but I was glad we didn't have to sleep together. His temper erupted just twice on the boat, a slap for something, and a hard shove for not walking fast enough in the lower passageway, knocking my head into an iron pole. Was he always like this?

I remembered going to Edmonton before we were married so I could meet his mother and sister. While having tea, Janet asked her mother if they should tell me about the dog, and her mother shook her head and quickly changed the subject. I'll give Janet credit for wanting to tell me something that had happened, involving Jack and a dog. Not a good something.

Later I wondered about the dog. And thought about it again many years later when Shannon Summers, my daughter Anne's friend, had her dog killed by a boy about their age.

Why didn't I say what was on the tip of my tongue: What did Jack do to the dog? Tell Janet what a nasty little social climber she was and how that little smile showed her for who she was? I lacked the courage. A lot of us did in the '50s. Afraid to rock the boat. I would protect myself, and if not saying what I wanted to say helped, I'd do it, but it wasn't easy. We were far from home when we crossed the Equator. The North Star was gone, as was the Big Dipper, replaced by the Southern Cross and other constellations. No Big Dipper. That really makes you feel homesick.

I was fascinated by the phosphorescent lights, like little cities at night just under the surface of the water, and remembered it years later while studying *Lord of the Flies*, the scene of poor Jack's beaten ten-year-old body floating out to sea surrounded by phosphorescence, honouring and loving him somehow. That scene made me cry.

Jack liked to explain things to me, like the phosphorescence and I loved to learn, which made me think it could have perhaps been a good match in that respect. If he didn't like to hit me. And if he liked to talk.

He had no patience for small talk and I have always believed that small talk is so underrated, it makes you feel a part of the human race. And I have always loved to make people laugh. It feels like one of my missions in life. My sense of humour had temporarily abandoned me.

The boat docked just once on the way down, at Savannah, Georgia. One of the sailors rowed us ashore.

We walked around an old residential area, I remember, big old houses, and everywhere the smothery greenery. Low-hanging fronds everywhere, huge flowering shrubbery, the air hot and moist, it was suffocating. I didn't think about the antebellum history of that city. The civil war. Only how to escape. I thought all the time about going home but no money and too much geography defeated me.

We came to an old cemetery, went in and walked around. As soon as we knew about the Savannah stopover I had started thinking of trying to get away. What I'd have done with no money I have no idea. In the cemetery Jack walked quite a way off to look at something and I ran, but there was no place to hide. Crouching behind a monument like a kid playing hide and seek, knowing it was stupid, and of course he found me. And laughed.

Not long after Savannah, we had a huge storm at sea, tossing the boat around like a toy boat in a bathtub with splashing kids. Everyone, including Jack, was violently seasick. For some reason I was not.

It was near dark when I made my way up the metal stairs, clinging to railings and posts, almost falling with every step, to the upstairs windows and looked out. I will never forget that sight.

Waves, I guess they're still called waves when they look about the height of a three-storey apartment block, the boat struggling up that wall of water, engine groaning, boat lurching, to the crest; seeming to hang there, then plunging down the other side. Water flooding the decks. The gigantic waves a radiant pale green in the boat's lights, oddly looking like they were lit from behind. It was exciting, and should have been terrifying, but wasn't. In my memory, it felt like I was looking at the boat as separate from me, as if I was watching it from somewhere close by. From inside of me, maybe.

There was a pole just outside the door. I wanted to feel the storm, close up, and very very carefully slid out, hanging on for dear life into the sound and fury, water rushing onto the deck and off again, the thunderous roar, the straining engine. I wasn't afraid, just excited. It wasn't outside of me now.

After about five minutes, one of the sailors in the wheelhouse, apparently shocked at the sight of me, grabbed and pulled me inside. I was soaked. It could have been pouring rain as well, but who could tell? I always remember the blond sailor was handsome, which is kind of funny in the circumstances.

I will never forget that night, watching the captain struggling to keep the ship upright. The unearthly green wall of water. It was like having a front row seat at the most exciting show on earth. Or at sea.

When the storm abated somewhat the same sailor took me inside and helped me get downstairs to the ugly sick bay.

Unfortunately, Jack was still alive.

Belem harbour was a vivid watercolour painting, hundreds of small fishing boats with brightly coloured sails. It felt so good to reach land I offered up a prayer of thanks.

We lived with another Canadian couple for several months before they went home. It was a suite rented to expats – you just carry in your suitcase and you're home. An expression only. Home was very far away.

Before the other couple left, we all went to a movie one night. As we waited in the crush of the lobby, there was a loud bang and a man who'd been standing with a beautiful woman between us and the other couple – fell to the floor, dead. There was some screaming and people running, but most, including us, stayed for the movie, though I couldn't take it in. It was a shocking introduction to Belem. The story in the paper said it was a crime of passion, the dead man was with the shooter's wife, and the implication was that he wouldn't be punished too harshly. If at all.

Jack was away often for a week at a time. The oil well was in the jungle, and that made it easier. I was soon pregnant, and felt horribly tired, though not throwing up for weeks, thank God. I learned a bit of Portuguese and ventured out, enjoying the colour and admiring the handsome, beautiful Brazilian people. Some election was coming up and noisy loudspeaker trucks with cheering people in the box waving banners were everywhere.

Almost every week we played bridge with another couple – a gregarious, warm-hearted Canadian woman called Betty who was married to a Portuguese doctor, Otto Hiltner. A lovely man.

And life went on. It felt like an unsteady holding pattern. Like something had to give.

Señor Cotta

I had too much time to pass and needed something to do.

Browsing around the shops one day I saw a high shelf displaying some very nice paintings. In my fractured Portuguese I managed to ask the shopkeeper about the artist – it was too high to see a signature. That is Señor Cotta, she said, proudly. Then I asked if she would know where I might get some art lessons and gave her my address. She just smiled so I thought she hadn't understood me.

The next afternoon the doorbell rang. I wasn't expecting anybody but opened the door. A short, dark man gave a little bow and smartly announced, I am Señor Cotta and I have come to give you art lessons. And he wasn't kidding. In no time I was having my first drawing lesson. We drew some apples with Señor Cotta guiding me to look at light and shadow, and declared himself quite pleased with my effort.

He was a very sweet man, and I felt totally comfortable

with him. He wanted to know where I lived and when I told him Canada, he shuddered to show me what he thought of that frigid place. When my drawing was finished, he asked if he should come back in a week, and when I said yes, please, he smiled. He had a beautiful smile. He charged next to nothing.

We had three more drawing lessons and when he said, We paint? I nodded vigourously. He pointed out the window and I said something like We go out and paint? and he nodded vigourously. And laughed. His English was quite good.

The next week he came for me and we boarded a bus. I had no idea where we were going but it didn't matter. The bus wasn't quite full but men were hanging on the outside like streamers, laughing and shouting at the passing cars. We got a seat together. People seemed to know Señor Cotta.

The men outside leapt off every so often, sometimes into the traffic, eliciting fist shaking and swearing – you can tell swearing in any language. The men laughed.

When we arrived at the entrance to a large park, Señor Cotta turned and smiled at me. You paint here, he said.

He asked me to pick a scene that I would like to try to paint. After walking around a bit, and laughing at the antics of monkeys in a large cage – one of them stole my earring – I picked a place where the trees leaned in on either side over a wide path with a sunny glade beyond.

He nodded and began to unpack the case he seemed to carry everywhere, it was like watching a magician as each thing emerged. A folding easel, a folding stool, a box with a stretched canvas inside, paints, easel, brushes rolled in a folding fan with thin bamboo ribs. It was amazing. I didn't use the stool, it felt better standing, and he approved that choice.

I actually produced a rather nice, small painting that more or less captured the distance and the sunny spot. The trees were also quite good. He was delighted.

Señor Cotta had some kind of box that would protect the picture and I carried it on the return trip. I felt happy with my picture. And being with Señor Cotta.

On our last lesson, it was raining and I worked on painting indoors. A still life with a coconut and some banana and oranges.

It was peaceful, with the rain falling outside, and the painting was almost done. Except for one thing. The coconut was smooth as a bowling ball.

Onde esta os cabelos de coco? I said, sending Señor Cotta into a laughing fit. He laughed so hard he almost fell off his chair.

Where is the hair of the coconut? I had asked.

No cabelos, I said mournfully, just to see him laugh some more.

When he had recovered he showed me how to put the hair on the coconut.

And that was the last time I saw that lovely little man, but I have thought of him often. He felt like a friend.

I'm sorry I couldn't say goodbye to him.

The Buzzard

Time went on. Pregnancy kept me safer, but not totally safe. Jack didn't need a reason. One very bad scene happened, witnessed by the cook, but after that it stopped. For some reason weight was falling off me and there wasn't much to spare. We didn't have a scale but my clothes were getting looser every day.

We continued to play bridge with Otto and Betty Hiltner. Well, they played bridge. I tried but would never be a bridge player, glad when I got to be the dummy. I saw Otto looking at me at times as if he wondered about my health.

Siesta. Nap time for old people, I'd thought at first, but I started to lie down to read at that time. There was no way to ignore the huge buzzard looking in the bedroom window. It was always there at that time. Hunched down on the red tile roof of the building next door. The buildings were close and it was looking right at me.

You won't get me, I always said, but some days I

wondered. It was absolutely still, only shifting its weight occasionally, its feathers bulging and settling, while never taking its eyes off me. Patience incarnate, it never slept.

Jack had been out in the field for a week when I fell asleep one day. Something woke me with a start. He was sitting on a chair near the foot of the bed. There was a gun in his hand. A pistol.

As soon as you get off that bed I'm going to blow your fucking brains out, he said.

Shock, terror, heart wanting out, *don't say anything, don't look scared, he wants you to.*

Silence.

Outside a loudspeaker truck drove slowly past.

As soon as you get up off that bed, he said again.

Especially since being pregnant, I woke up needing the bathroom. I stood it as long as I could until I couldn't. *I'm not going to wet the bed to please you.*

I have to pee, I said. And somehow managed to stand up and walk past him on shaky legs and out of the room. In the bathroom across the hall I collapsed across the toilet, legs useless, locking the door from my knees. Whispering thank you God, thank you God, thank you God, the toilet my altar.

After no sound for a very long time, I heard him walk past the door. Not knowing if he was still in the suite. I didn't dare leave the bathroom.

Finally, finally I screwed up the courage to creep out, heart racing. It was dark. He wasn't there.

I slept in the bathroom. The door locked.

The next day Otto's office called to say Doctor Hiltner wanted to see me.

I'm very concerned about you, he said. I know what's going on with you and if you don't go home you aren't going to live very long.

It sounded like the most wonderful thing anyone

ever said to me. For someone to know. To acknowledge it. I told him about the day before and he just nodded. I want to see what you weigh, he said.

At five foot six and a half the scale stopped at ninety-eight pounds. I had lost twenty-five pounds.

You must go, as soon as possible. I will speak to Jack.

But how...thinking of the ticket.

I will take care of it, he said.

It was a beautiful day out and I walked home incredibly, wonderfully happy. I passed a shop with a pair of red wedge sandals with rope soles in the window and I went in and bought them. In another shop I bought a cream-coloured linen coat, a real classic. Then stopped at an open air coffee place and sat with a cup of strong coffee – also wonderful, though I had never liked Brazilian coffee – feeling the big fear-filled place inside fill with gratitude. Gratitude and love for Doctor Otto. And maybe, just maybe, the tiniest sliver of concern for Jack, who was a sick man. A very sick man. God knows how he managed his rages at the oil well.

I was going home to that little house in the small town of Ruddell, Saskatchewan, where my parents, who were worried about me, lived now. To safety.

I was pregnant, but that didn't matter, we would be safe.

Both of us.

Hurricane Hazel

Two days later I stood in the airport waiting room, with Otto, Betty, and Jake The Crocodile Man. Jake, a short, husky man with a big smile, always wore a hat with a crocodile hatband, and crocodile boots. He hunted and bought the big animals from everywhere and sold them to businesses that made purses, shoes, boots, and whatever anyone wanted crocodilian. He also owned an expat store where you could buy anything – Players cigarettes, rye whisky, special marmalade and shortbread for the Brits, anything people from away yearned for.

Jake is going to watch out for you, Otto said, and Jake beamed at me. Someone near us mentioned a hurricane heading somewhere, and Jake said, no worry, not coming anywhere near.

On the plane, Jake had the aisle seat across from mine, and every time I looked over he smiled. It was comforting. Once I saw him checking his watch, one of those big, black waterproof ones, and wondered if he was getting off soon, no crocodiles in New York.

The plane was pretty old, and while the big door to the great blue yonder wasn't taped shut, it looked like it should be. The steward had a little cubbyhole where he often retreated to squirt something up his nose, I could see him from my seat. He looked very pale, hung over, I thought. Or maybe addicted to the stuff.

My left arm, which had received a vaccination the day before, was getting warm and red.

Our first stop was French Guiana, where anyone without a vaccination certificate had to get off the plane. I didn't have mine, and couldn't remember where I put it, not realizing you had to present it anywhere. My arm, still sporting the needle hole, did not help. No certificate, another vaccination. In the same arm.

At the next stop, British Guiana, Jake got off, after almost taking my hand with him he shook it so hard, and he was gone. Crocodiles were waiting.

Several more people got on, a friendly black woman in Jake's seat, and the steward came to me with a little old lady in tow. This is Mrs. DeFraetes, he said. She is eighty-one years old and is traveling to Toronto. She is very nervous about the flight and we would like you to look after her. Put her under your wing, so to speak.

And thus began my odyssey with Mrs DeFraetes.

She told me she was going to Toronto to live with her son. Her husband, John, had died a few months before. In addition to her purse and hat, she had a large bag of knitting and a large round metal tin, a fruitcake for her son.

I held her hand and talked to her when we took off and we got through that without too much anxiety on her part. She had lived in British Guiana, now just Guyana, ever since she'd married, probably about sixty years. She relaxed more and took her knitting out of the bag, a wine-coloured sweater big enough for a gorilla, and began to knit. It made me wonder about her son.

The woman in Jake's seat was from Chicago, married to a doctor there. She'd been visiting family. I was glad she was there. A friendly presence. And all was as it should be. For a while.

The ride was getting rough, seatbelt signs lit. We progressed from rough to quite rough to holy shit! way too fast, loose things falling from the overhead bins, rosaries coming out everywhere, I wished I had one. It was like a giant angry hand was shaking the plane, up, down, sideways. *Are you sorry now? Take that! And that!*

Mrs. De Fraetes was surprisingly quiet, eyes closed, scared speechless maybe.

Then we dropped.

Straight down. Fast.

OHHHHHHHHH... OHHHHHHHHHH... A loud chorus of fear went up. My stomach surged into my throat.

We dropped like something off a table. Straight down, but still horizontal, thank God.

Still falling. Heading for the ocean. Screams. Crying. Someone behind shouting, No! No! Loud creaks and thuds, like the plane was falling apart.

This is it, I thought, holding Mrs DeFraetes's hand. Mom and Dad will be devastated. I felt strangely calm, maybe that's what dying is.

Then slowly, ever, ever, so slowly, the descent slowed, and finally the plane made a wide turn. The screaming stopped.

The pilot's voice came on. Sorry, folks, we weren't expecting that. We hit the edge of Hurricane Hazel, She's a big one. We're cleared to land in San Juan, Puerto Rico, but we need to stay up until it's safe to land. And it might be a rough one.

The woman across from me reached over and grabbed my hand and squeezed it and we laughed and cried. It felt amazing.

How is your seat-mate?

Looking bewildered, but I think she's good. How are you, Mrs. DeFraetes?

Fine, I think. She was still wearing her hat.

We laughed. She's a trouper, I said.

You look like you could use a drink, and I could. Want to put her to bed in the hotel and meet me in the bar? I could tell she was a seasoned traveler.

That sounded so normal. Thank God for normal.

After about an hour of air taxiing – or maybe it just seemed that long – the pilot came on. We're running low on gas and are going to land. It's raining heavily and our landing is going to be rough, so hang on.

I didn't see any lights out the window till we were almost down, it looked like we were landing in the ocean. After a wildly bumpy landing, the plane stopped and we clapped and cheered, the ones who weren't paralyzed. The pilot made a brief appearance, grinning broadly, and we cheered like crazy. I fell in love with him on the spot and am sure I wasn't the only one.

We disembarked into a wall of water, like we were under a waterfall. We were both wearing coats, Mrs. D and I, sopping wet by the time we were inside and were led to an airport hotel. I got Mrs. D dried off and into bed. She was asleep before she hit the pillow.

Hanging our dripping coats in the shower, I saw how red and swollen my arm had become. I'd managed to forget it while we were going to die up there. Facing death – or believing you are – focuses the mind, someone said. I put on lipstick and headed for the bar.

Brazilian people are handsome, but Puerto Rican people are beautiful. Tall, strong, warm-skinned, beautiful-featured people, and I thought, not for the first or last time, that white people must look pretty inferior to a lot of the world. White, pug-nosed, stringy-haired, pale-eyed people, whatever made us think we were so hot?

Case in point. I saw a black arm waving and wove my way over to a tiny table. She stood up and hugged me, careful of my arm.

Sit down, honey, and tell me what you want to drink. I want to know all about you, she said. And about the old lady.

She reached in her purse and brought out a bottle of aspirin, I never leave home without it, take two for your arm and have a drink. She was almost as old as my mother and it was comforting. You see a doctor as soon as you land, she said, that arm looks infected.

We had two drinks and talked for about an hour. I told her about my American dad and about asking him about Chickago. That made her laugh. I liked her accent, not southern of course, but with hints of that, a Chicago accent. She knew I was pregnant and said I don't know what you've been through, honey, but I know it wasn't good and you need to take very good care of yourself. Very, very good care.

I had my first introduction to a unisex bathroom. I entered just as a tall man was zipping up, and at my sputtered apology he did a jokey little bow, sweeping his arm toward the cubicles. All the same, dear, all the same, he said with a big, blindingly white smile. I'd have to tell Dad about him, and about my friend from Chickago.

Suddenly I couldn't wait to see my mother. Dad, too, of course, but I wanted my mom. Wanted her to tuck me in bed. Rub my feet. Rub my forehead, except

160

every time she did that, it made me cry. All my life, for some reason.

My new temporary friend and I checked the next day's tentative departure time and said goodnight. Mrs. DeFraetes was snoring as I crawled gratefully into the other bed, not able to sleep for a while, my arm burning, memories of the flight.

The airport lineup at the ticket counter the next day was very long, Mrs. Defraetes, who seemed a bit vague this morning, standing close by. When I finally had boarding passes in my hand, we didn't have much time, I turned to collect her.

She wasn't there.

She was nowhere in the lineup or anywhere I could see, running though the airport. I ran to the washrooms, no Mrs. DeFraetes. Not sitting on any seats anywhere. We had to board soon. Very soon, I saw, looking at the passes.

I grabbed a uniformed airport guy and asked for help. He hadn't seen her. We ran everywhere inside, and I checked the toilets again. Maybe she's outside, he said, I doubted it but we ran out. She wasn't there.

Is that her? He pointed to a swimming pool some distance away, but apparently part of the airport.

It was her. Sitting on the side of the pool, dangling her legs in the water.

Come on, he said.

Her shoes were neatly lined up beside her, her stockings, too, and her hat. Mrs. DeFraetes, we have to go. The plane is leaving.

That's all right, dear, I'm not going. John told me to wait here for him.

John, oh God. Her dead husband, I whispered to the airport guy.

He pulled her out of the water and put her down in a poolside chair. I struggled to pull her stockings on over her wet legs. He put on her shoes, tied up the laces, and put her hat on.

I grabbed her purse. Let's go, he said, and we clasped our hands behind her shoulders, lifted her off her feet and ran.

We made it. I thanked that wonderful man, so grateful to him. Got a nice big smile and a Good Luck back. And we were on our way again. Mrs. DeFraetes looking a bit like she'd been dragged through a knothole.

I'm sorry, Mrs. DeFraetes, don't worry, we have just one little plane ride and you're going to see your son. Today. That turned out to be a big, fat lie, but fortunately neither of us knew it.

Mrs. D's knitting was in the bag, missing one needle. She was knitting when the plane dropped. I hoped we wouldn't see someone with a knitting needle sticking out the side of the head. Amazingly, the fruitcake tin was intact.

We both slept for a while, then had coffee and a sandwich as the trip got quite bumpy, spilling coffee on my skirt.

Seatbelt lights again. Clouds outside navy blue to black. Our seat was right beside the left wing and I saw a bright white light hit the wing tip, crackle along the wing and felt it crackle down the body toward the tail and disappear.

What was that?

The pilot's voice came on. We were hit by lightning, but don't worry, it's gone. Lightning won't damage the plane. We're grounded.

But the ride was getting quite rough, and continued that way. I had no idea then of course how widespread Hurricane Hazel had been and some of the storms in its wake were no weaklings either.

I don't know how long later there was an announcement that passengers for Toronto would have to stop over in New York. We had missed our connection because of the storm.

I wanted to cry. I had no money for a hotel and probably Mrs D didn't either. I'd heard that airlines supply hotel rooms when they miss a connection, but I was exhausted and just wanted to get home. And I had no faith we'd even see New York without another Happening. The hallelujah chorus, maybe. Jesus looking in the window.

We landed, finally, Mrs. D and I, our suitcases which took awhile to find, the knitting bag and the fruitcake. We went to the airline office and were told by a large, bald man at a desk that they would not pay for a hotel. I explained about Mrs. DeFraetes's age, that we'd been through a hurricane, were exhausted and had no money for a hotel.

You're not getting a hotel. And he went back to working at something.

After a while he looked up. You can sit there all night, you're not getting a hotel.

We sat there. Us and our suitcases, and coats, Mrs. D's hat, the knitting bag and the fruitcake.

If you don't leave, I will call security and have you removed, he said.

We didn't leave.

Jesus Christ! he said, grabbing the phone and ordering a cab. He got our names and called a hotel.

The cab driver had the window down all the way and a very cold wind blew on us as he drove at breakneck speed to a distant hotel – I caught a cold before we got there – where they checked us into two rooms.

I managed to get Mrs. D to bed and then looked in her purse to see if there was a phone number for her son in Toronto. There was, and I called, telling the nice worried-sounding man who answered what had happened and to be prepared for his mother's mind to be a bit confused by all the stress. I gave him the time of our arrival, without much confidence that we'd actually get there the next day. Then I went to the other room, arranged a wakeup call, and crashed.

The phone rang. Time to get up already? Dragging myself conscious.

Are you traveling with a little old woman?

Yes. Why?

She's running around the halls in her nightgown.

She was.

Come on, Mrs. DeFraetes, you have to get some sleep.

No. Where are we?

We're in a hotel and in the morning we're going to Toronto.

She let me put her to bed again.

Crash. Sleep.

The phone.

She's doing it again, we can't have her running around up there. Something might happen to her.

Like maybe I'd strangle her, I thought.

Are you going to stay in bed and go to sleep?

Yes.

Do you promise?

Yes.

Cross your heart?

Yes. Did she look a bit sly?

Crash. Ring.

Okay, sorry. I'll take her into bed with me.

I went to sleep with my hand on her hip, deciding if she woke up I'd go with her and run around the halls. She slept, and even her snoring couldn't keep me awake.

Getting in a cab with our purses, two suitcases, Mrs. DeFraetes, her hat – I didn't know why she didn't keep it on her head – the knitting bag and the fruitcake, we headed for Idlewild Airport. That's what it was called before it became the John F. Kennedy Airport.

I hung on to Mrs. D while I got our boarding passes. When I turned around my suitcase with my wonderful linen coat on top was gone. My red shoes, too. I could have cried, checking her suitcase.

Better hurry, ladies, said the ticket agent, you don't have much time. I grabbed Mrs. D and ran – well, trotted, Mrs. D's fastest pace – to the gate. Partway there I dropped the tin. The lid came off and the fruit-cake rolled around the dirty airport floor, breaking into pieces, which Mrs. DeFraetes tried to get back in the can. I had to pull her away and keep going. Now we both wanted to cry. We'd had enough, both of us, and then some. Poor little Mrs. D. Poor me, too, I thought. I felt awful, the cold gone straight to my chest. The arm had gone down a bit, and was less painful.

Her son and daughter-in-law were nice people, and her beautiful granddaughter, or great-granddaughter. Her son wanted to buy me lunch but there was only time for coffee.

But I got to witness Mrs D's return to sanity. Once she saw her son the whole awful experience fell away from her like a nightmare she'd never remember, and she looked happy. And, well, *with it*. We hugged and I caught the plane to Saskatoon, landing there some-time in the afternoon.

Mrs. Wylie and her son, Jackie, were in the bus depot, going back to Mervin. Jackie had thrown up on me in the car when we went to see the queen at Biggar. Jackie was a man, now, with the mind of a child, still. Mrs. Wylie talked and I listened a bit, too tired to talk. I told her I'd been in Toronto, which was true after all.

It was a long wait. The bus didn't leave for hours.

Finally, it came. I said goodnight to Mrs. Wylie and

Jackie, sitting together near the front of the bus as they had probably done many times before, and falling onto the long seat at the back, went out like a light.

I woke to a hand shaking my shoulder, an alarmed face.

Oh, thank God the bus driver said, I've been trying to wake you for ages. I thought you were dead.

The bus didn't normally go into the little town of Ruddell but he drove me right to the house, and around to the kitchen door, me lurching half asleep behind him. I think he was afraid if he left me off on the highway, I'd fall asleep in the ditch.

I couldn't believe it. The long, long, long journey was over. My odyssey with Mrs. DeFraetes done, she was home safe, and so was I. So were we.

The house was dark but the door wasn't locked, it never was. My dad, wakened by my entrance, came into the kitchen. He looked like he was seeing a ghost. A weeping ghost. I realized later it wasn't just surprise at my appearance, it was my appearance.

My mother woke up and hugged me tight, I didn't want to let go.

They decided to talk tomorrow, and that was good. Mom changed the sheets on their double bed and I have never felt anything half so wonderful again as that bed. I slept for twenty-four hours. Mom kept checking on me, she said, not believing anybody could sleep that long.

Five months later my daughter, Anne, was born.

North Battleford

Saskatoon

CJNB
Marriage
Teddy
Anne Szumigalski
Victoria
Finding a Family
Going On
Westgate Books
Auntie Eva Knitting
Bowled Over by Poems
Auntie the Play
You Can't Miss It. Cows.
Mining for Stories
Unknowables
You Can't Miss It. Cookies.
Wonderful Times
The OBC
Betty Lee and Oliver
You Can't Miss It: Wild Rose Country.
Meeting Sgt. Wilson
Trip to Scotland
Stories I Missed
Meeting Got To Go
You Can't Miss it: Paynton.
Unknowables. Ghosts.
What I'm Trying to Say Is Goodbye

CJNB

When my daughter Anne was two, I got an office job at Macdonald Lumber in North Battleford. I rented a small basement suite and hired a wonderful woman, Mrs. Wade, to take care of Anne while I was at work. I was beginning my new life. Our new lives together.

I didn't want to work there long because of the man who couldn't keep his hands to himself. The other woman who worked there and I would call for each other if we needed to use the washroom downstairs, to avoid him lurking outside the door. Stuff women hated but sometimes had to put up with then. And still do. So when I saw an ad for someone in the advertising department at Radio Station CJNB I ran over on a lunch break and filled out an application. Harry Dekker, the manager, called the next day. I was hired to write radio ads. Harry Dekker was a great boss and his morning show was a hit all over the province and beyond.

Working at CJNB was amazing. The continuity

department consisted of Ross Miller, a young, very funny guy from Toronto, and me. Someone must have given me some training but I don't remember who. We talked to advertisers who came in, or phoned, to tell us what they wanted on air, what length, and on which program, if possible, they wanted the ads read. I loved, loved, loved that job. Trying to find original ideas for ads was fun, and I was good at it. We tried ideas out on each other, some of them pretty off-the-wall, others hilarious, and we laughed a lot. My first writing job. Arlene Cole was soon added to the department and also became a friend.

Louise Tetrault, a great receptionist, became my friend too. We hung out together and dated as couples. We spent some weekends at my parents' cabin at Days Beach on Jackfish Lake, Arlene also. And never without Anne. She stayed with my parents there sometimes while I worked. They adored her and it was mutual.

CJNB at that time was in a rundown warehouse above a large furniture store in North Battleford, and they were part of a once-in-a-lifetime staff with Harry Dekker, the boss everyone loved. Guys whistling down the halls and dropping in to bum a cigarette – red-haired Lee Sage, especially – and chat. Lee once lent me his gas lighter to light my cigarette and I accidentally turned up the flame while lighting his, singeing off half his well-known red moustache.

Jimmy Oxman, an announcer, was skinny, dark-haired, very funny. He did a lot of convincing imitations of animal sounds, if you heard a rooster crowing or cow mooing somewhere in the building you knew it was Jimmy. It sounded like a zoo when he was in the music library next door. These guys knew and loved their music and chose what they wanted on their programs.

Lawence Branter, married, all around good guy,

had the farm show. He wished his wife "Happy Anniversary" on air since he'd forgotten it before and was afraid to go home. He had a great wife. Elva. He also gave the hospital report. I can hear his deep voice saying a patient is *up and about the ward*; another *had surgery and is doing well*; and someone else *is ready to go home tomorrow and needs a ride*. Families were happy when they heard their loved one was *up and about the ward*.

Sometimes I say when asked how I am when I've been ill, Oh, I'm up and about the ward.

Eileen Risling, a good friend of Louise's and a very funny woman, was the only female announcer. I never got to know Eileen as well as I'd have liked to, I think she left to get married not long after I started work there.

Louise and Eileen had a very funny experience driving home from Saskatoon. Eileen really needed to pee and it was a long way to the next town, when she spied an outhouse, a real toilet, not a mirage, on the edge of a farmer's field. She slammed on the brakes, ran through the ditch, climbed over the fence, ran to the outhouse and yanked open the door. The farmer was sitting there, large legs bare. She slammed the door, ran back, climbed the fence, ran through the ditch and into the car and sped off, laughing and laughing. They must have laughed all the way home.

I used that in my first novel, I couldn't resist it.

Ron Smith, a young man with impeccable manners and a kind heart, would go on to manage CBC Television in Calgary.

CJNB lucked into Bob Hildebrand, a super smart guy, great voice, arrived from the east, CBC I think. He had married a devout Catholic woman who kept trying – not to convert him since I don't think he was anything else – to get him into the fold. He resisted fiercely. I remember working over Christmas one year and going into the control room to give Bob an ad. He was in a mood. Jesus Christ! he said, I was at Midnight Mass last night and some bingo player puked down the back of my neck. Ruined my suit jacket. Unmentionable words here.

Apparently he wasn't kneeling and the bingo player was. I didn't laugh till I got back in my office.

Don Brown, handsome Chinese announcer, was married to a very pretty blonde woman. When I think of Don this comes to mind: I was trying to get the shoulder attachment to stay on my phone, it was necessary to leave your hands free to write while talking to customers. Frustrated by it falling off yet again, I was taping it to the phone with unnecessary force when the tape snapped and the phone slammed my forehead hard. Dizzy and feeling a lump rising fast, I staggered out to the mirror over the sink in the hall across from two toilet cubicles. A huge red lump the size of a small potato was blooming on my forehead. I stood there stunned as Don Brown came whistling down the corridor and, catching sight of me, yelled ACGH!, dove into the toilet and threw up. That didn't help.

Sometimes it was dangerous work. I was bending over talking to Ross when he laughed and reached up to pull my head down, just joking around, when a shot rang out – pardon the cliché – and an air rifle bullet stuck in the wall right behind me.

Al Ridell, engineer, was another very witty guy and incorrigible punster. We were all at Jimmy Oxman's cabin at the lake for a party and Louise and I had to go out to the outdoor toilet. We passed Al sitting on the back step, smoking. It was dark in the toilet and we were laughing, I can't find a hole, Louise said. It's uncanny, said a voice from the dark. I remember seeing Bob Hildebrand, who was drunk, glaring at the crucifix on the wall, and hoping he wasn't going to do something stupid.

An older man whose name I've forgotten was the salesman, out pitching the advantages of having the name of your business on air, and often chatting up Louise at reception.

The guys had nicknames for us women – Louise was Fifi, I forget the others, all sexy names and I was Big Lois, obviously the madame. I don't think there are many jobs with so much laughter. Most of the staff were still single, in that great place in life still free of encumbrances and in love with the job you do every day. Harry Dekker knew he had a creative crew and was a hands-off boss and a very funny man.

After a year I was promoted to editor and given a raise.

Sometimes it was difficult trying to figure out what our customers were trying to get across in an ad. The manager of the city's best menswear store wanted an ad for some new and exciting underwear. What's so great about it? I asked.

Everything. And I want you to say, and he paused for effect, You Can Tell Before You Get It Home. I think he was disappointed when I didn't applaud.

"You can tell before you get it home?" What does that mean?

It means what it says. You can tell before you get it home.

What can you tell? That it's super comfortable? Doesn't ride up?

I don't understand your problem.

How can you know, unless you wear it home?

He looked offended. And he was a very good customer, they spent lots of money on ads. I think he thought I was making fun of him. Maybe a little.

Okay, You Can Tell Before You Get It Home.

He nodded.

You want to end with that?

Yes, please.

What the hell does this mean? Bob Hildebrand, waving the ad.

He's in love with it. Harry says okay. So we let the listeners try to figure it out.

I did, however, redeem myself with the nice menswear manager. He was also a Kinsman and in charge of ads for their new bingo.

I wish I had a catchy name for it, he said longingly, sitting on the edge of my desk.

Kingo.

You'd have thought I'd written *The Rise and Fall.* Or invented the light bulb.

They used North Battleford Kinsmen Kingo for at least twenty years, I think, and maybe still do. My claim to fame.

A fantastic job. Very smart, funny people who respected and enjoyed each other and all knew they had something special.

I did an on-air bit when the women told jokes for some reason. Harry asked me after it if I'd consider an onair job but I declined. The thought made me nervous.

And I also wanted to be with my daughter more while she was little. Mom and Dad took her to Ruddell or the lake every so often, but I was starting to want to settle down.

That's when I met Lyle Simmie, a smart, sociable, divorced man with two children, four and five years old. He was a contractor, planning to move to Saskatoon to build a large trailer park. I decided to go along.

Marriage

When we married we had a ready-made family: Odell, five; Leona, four; and Anne, three. We had gone to Regina so I could meet his parents and the kids, looked after by their grandparents. Odell climbed onto my lap and leaned back against me. That was it for me. His hands were so chapped I wanted to ask his grandma, Jake, for some lotion but didn't want it to seem like a criticism. Jake's real name was Louise, but she had been a Jacobs before marriage and the nickname stuck. Leona, freckled with wildly curly blonde hair, was not impressed and kicked me in the leg. She was her dad's girl and a bit jealous. All three children had problems – anger, shyness, jealousy – behaviours to be expected, but gradually things smoothed out.

I will never forget the first time I made Odell laugh so hard. I was sitting on the cupboard, over the sink, talking to the kids about something, and I said, So pay attention to Big Chief Bum-in-the-Sink. He fell down laughing, rolling on the floor. I loved to make that kid laugh.

And he made me laugh, too. He once went into the bathroom just when Anne stepped out of tub after a bath with Leona. Gee, Mom, are girls ever plain, he said.

And once coming home from school through the backyard he saw me through the kitchen window holding up a raw chicken and burning off the pin-feathers with a flaming twist of paper. He stopped, looked and tore into the house. It's going to take a long time to cook the chicken like that, he informed me.

Lyle was building a trailer park and the three men who worked for him ate a noon meal with us. I didn't poison anyone anyway, and one of my nicest memories is when Odell, as an adult, said, I often think of those good meals we had. That meant a lot. Scott was born two years after we married and we all adored him.

At first we rented two old two-storey houses. The one on 9th Street had a hideous kitchen with a very low stone sink. I cried when I saw it. We bought our first home, a bungalow on Macdonald Crescent in Greystone Heights, and eventually had a two-storey house built on Rutter Crescent in the West Greystone area.

We all loved that house. We made friends, the kids made friends and life went on. We had many happy years in that house on Rutter Crescent as the kids grew and developed their own interests – two athletes, Leona and Odell, one artist, Anne, and Scott, child-actor-all-around-entertainer. I spent a lot of time driving him to rehearsals at the university, Castle Theatre, and Persephone Theatre. He was a natural, he could even cry on cue. There was always a coloured picture of Anne's on the wall somewhere. Odell won the provincial wrestling championship in high school. Leona was a talented runner and speed skater till a bad fall wrecked her knee. I didn't realize how bad it was at first. That sports were over for her. A terrible, life-changing blow. I think now we didn't support her as much as we should have. Her practices were always at night. Lyle, selling real estate now – he loved it – was working evenings now, and someone had to be home with the kids.

I think there was an unspoken agreement when we married. You look after the children and the house and I will give you a nice home. We both fulfilled those roles but it was far from a loveless marriage. I gave Lyle a wedding ring when we'd been married five years.

The kids had such freedom then. Anne and her friends rode their bikes to the university barns to make rounds with the man who looked after the barns and who seemed not to mind a retinue of ten-and-eleven-year-old animal-loving girls. Unfortunately, that wouldn't happen now.

We especially loved time spent at Days Beach on Jackfish Lake where the kids hitched a ride every day with the Days Garden horse-drawn wagon loaded with fresh vegetables for sale. Corn in season. They looked forward to weekends when their dad was there. Lyle was a workaholic so those weekends were precious. Boating – never a favourite of mine – water skiing – ditto – barbecues – Lyle made the most incredibly delicious barbecued chicken – sunning on the beach when the kids were swimming out to the diving platform. I once again impressed with my ability to float without moving a muscle. We sometimes had friends out from town.

Scott was accident-prone at the lake – falling and rolling down the big cactus-covered hill at Cochin, that was terrible; stepping his bare foot on a live coal from the barbecue, also terrible. When he was very young he couldn't get to sleep in the top bunk, he was afraid of the cobwebs. We removed the cobwebs.

We were squatters in a trailer at the back of my parents' waterfront cottage, which I still dream of sometimes, so I got to spend quite a lot of time with Mom. My dad had died before this time. Lyle added a large room onto the trailer, and built a wonderful stone fireplace. He was happy doing that. We were impressed.

We were there during the moon landing, Lyle up on the roof trying to get the aerial on the small TV working, all of us calling back and forth – that's good! No, no, it's gone. What can you see? Nothing, no, do what you did before! There! There! Ooops. We did see enough to say we saw it.

We took trips to Banff, Vancouver, Victoria, Seattle, and others, often taking Mom. In our search for a good motel we once forgot Scott at a motel office in Vancouver. We missed him almost immediately but he's never let me forget it. I also left him at the hairdresser's once when he was three. I remember pulling into our driveway, reversing fast, speeding back, my heart in my mouth. Only a few blocks. He was sitting on the front desk enjoying the attention of the admiring hairdressers when I frantically returned. He's so cute! they said, and he was. And I adored him. He was such a smart, delightfully funny kid. And, as Anne said recently, he was universally adored.

My hairdresser at the time was Len Cyr, a lovely man who left us in the lurch to join the priesthood. I've often thought of writing a story about a hairdresser turned priest and the woman who missed him so much, and his little lectures to her about sins against her hair, that she became a Catholic so she could go to him for confession.

I got a second-hand sewing machine intending to make clothes for the girls. Almost all their clothes, I was sure. It was exciting. I started with dresses for Leona and Anne and it almost drove me mad. The dresses were nice but not worth having a nervous breakdown over. Every time I looked at that sewing machine I felt guilty, finally ripping up the patterns and shamefully relegating the sewing machine to the basement, replacing it with an easel. My new passion. I also took pottery lessons from Bjorg Hedemann down the street. Lyle was good-humoured about it all. Someone said, What is a dilettante but an artist searching for an art form?

My friend Alice Carpenter and I made sketching trips to the country and it was great. We always laughed a lot when we were together. Those were very good times in our family and our marriage.

Some time after my experience of making dresses for the girls, I must have forgotten how much I hated sewing. So when the Co-op store offered "Make Your Very Own Mannequin," I signed up.

The group of women, all experienced seamstresses except for me, gathered under the guidance of Mrs. Helene Ducey, a large, no-nonsense employee and television personality with a show where she told women how to do things better. How to fold fitted sheets, for one. I failed that.

Mrs. Ducey gave us a list of things to buy: a yard and a half of surgical gauze tubing; a roll of wide brown paper tape and – this Mrs. Ducey stressed – *a good girdle*, it was a *necessity*! I had an indifferent girdle and paid a whole fifteen dollars for a state-of-the-art girdle.

We divided into teams of three. One stripped to bra

and girdle and pulled on the gauze tubing. Mrs. Ducey then pulled a tape around our waists so tightly we bulged over and under, which continued to distress Mrs. Ducey, valiantly pushing and pulling and trying to eliminate our bulges during the whole exercise. Good luck with that.

The two others then set to work wetting the tape and applying it tightly over the gauze and the body beneath in all its hills and valleys, some in the wrong places. Then you stood, hardly able to breathe, while it hardened. One woman fainted. Mrs. Ducey telling us Lift her up! Lift her up! on the table. Careful now, careful, don't bump her, more concerned about the mannequin in progress than why the woman was out cold. But it wasn't long before Mrs. Ducey had her up again. She looked ready to fall over, but didn't dare. I think Mrs. Ducey was involved in real estate also, very successfully. *I hate this house but Mrs. Ducey made me buy it!*

When we were ready, Mrs. Ducey produced scissors with the longest blades I'd ever seen and proceeded to cut the body armor up the back where it was slapped together with more sticky tape. When my turn came, I felt the cold blade and a *zip!* as my state of the art girdle raced around me. Or tried to. Not enough room.

Our mannequins were lined up on the table. The mannequin of the plainest, shyest woman in the group – she may have been Mennonite – looked really hot. Others not so much.

A couple of days later when I saw our next-door neighbour and friend Hank Eisler, who owned a successful insurance company, out in the yard, I said, Hank, what insurance should you claim for having your girdle cut off in public?

I'd have to know more details, Hank replied.

After one more indifferent production we moved the sewing machine to the basement again. This time for good. Odell, a teen then with a basement bedroom, painted the mannequin red and used it as a room decoration.

These were very good years. The kids were older but not yet far into the teens, and I had more time to do things. And we loved where we lived.

Rutter Crescent was almost all young families with one exception, retired George and Helen Field who lived across the street and next door to the large Radostits family. I never saw George get in his car without first getting down on his knees and checking for kids under and behind his car. George and Helen were older but we all loved them and invited them to parties. George told me once about the first time he saw Helen. He was a young man washing the outside windows at the University President's house and fell in love when he saw Helen working in the kitchen. A lovely story. And a long, happy marriage. What could be better than that?

Several families got together for parties and barbecues in the summer, children included. While the kids ran around doing what kids do, the adults enjoyed a few drinks. Lyle had a glassed-in gazebo with a red fireplace built onto the back of the house. I once dropped a frozen roast on a glass topped table there and smashed it. I thought of the story about a woman who kills her husband with a frozen roast and when the police come it's sizzling away in the oven. Smells good, one policeman said.

There were Christmas and New Years parties, birthday parties, and "just because you felt like it" parties. Quite a lot of alcohol was consumed with apparently no problems. We started to have drinks when Lyle came home from work and would sometimes ask another couple to join us, and it was all very enjoyable.

Until it wasn't any more.

I was thirty-eight when alcohol became a problem for me. Bad hangovers. Worrying that I'd made a fool of myself. No, not at all, it's all in your head, they said. You're too funny to be an alcoholic, I heard that a lot, but it didn't help. Horrible headaches, throwing up. Not funny at all. Forgetting bits of the evening. I tried to quit many times but failed.

I know now that social drinkers don't have to stop drinking. And that women are much more vulnerable to becoming alcoholic than men. And you don't have to make a fool of yourself at parties, or leave your children to frequent bars to be an alcoholic, but it does damage to the family regardless.

I was afraid that my "loving everybody" syndrome that started with my first drink would create problems. Alice and I always went out for a New Year's drink and, once, seeing a man who looked very lonely, invited him to join us for a drink. He had just arrived from some other country and I invited him to our New Year's Eve party the next night. It wasn't long before I knew I wanted nothing to do with him, and every time the doorbell rang that New Year's Eve I was afraid to open the door. He knew our address, and had asked about my family. We started getting ugly phone calls, threatening our daughters.

Depressed and scared and ashamed, I sat on a bench at the Exhibition Grounds Corral watching Anne exercise her horse. She was the only person there and so vulnerable. I made a decision sitting on that bench. I was going to stop drinking. I didn't know for sure I was alcoholic but it had to stop. An appointment with a psychiatrist left me with no doubts.

The psychiatrist, a rather small man across the desk, was dressed entirely in green. Green suit, green shirt, green tie, even, when I glanced down, green shoes and socks under his desk. It was very distracting. Thinking that someday I'd like to write about him made it hard to concentrate, but I managed to blurt out I think I might have a problem with alcohol.

He looked at me – maybe I only imagined his eyes were green – and said, Have you ever had a blackout?

A blackout? I said. Is that where you can't remember parts of an evening when you are drinking?

That's a blackout.

Yes. I have blackouts.

Only alcoholics have blackouts, he said.

Thud.

Are you sure?

Positive. And it will only get worse.

Is alcohol a depressant?

Oh, yes. It most assuredly is.

I got up, thanked him, shook his hand, and left.

I walked out of his office and out of that building happier than I'd been for a long time. I had the answer. He had confirmed what I already knew deep down. I was an alcoholic. From now on my life was going to be different.

It was December 15, 1970. I have never had a drink since that day.

Thank you, Doctor Green. And I'm sorry. I did write about you.

It was not easy. Especially with Christmas looming. I hadn't finished getting gifts, and Lyle's parents and brother, Cork, and his wife, Eleanor, and their two-year-old, who invented the term terrible twos, were coming to stay. Lyle and Cork did their holiday drinking in the basement ping-pong room, so that helped, but of course alcohol was around. Their parents were shopping for a house in Saskatoon and argued a lot. The terrible-two smeared chocolate on the furniture and the drapes and screamed a lot, and it was a constant battle to stop her from turning the basement doorknob and falling downstairs.

I had to go out for coffee Christmas day with someone else who found the season difficult, just go out, walk, smoke, after the turkey was in the oven, and whenever I was sorely tempted. Cork's wife Eleanor was great. She knew what I was going through and took care of things. Drinks of cold water helped.

But with a powerful desire and a goal, and support from Lyle and my good friends, neighbours and others, the days became weeks became months. Sobriety became a way of life. I am grateful every day.

I had been writing short stories and sold a story to the radio program *Saskatchewan Short Stories*. I had wanted to write since I fell in love with a poem in grade four. This story, "Your Roses are Beautiful," was my first sale, but not the last to that program. I would be forty in a couple of years and wanted to do what I knew I was meant to do before it was too late. Thank you, Doctor Green.

The following summer, six months sober, I was accepted at the Saskatchewan Summer School of the Arts for a two-week writing program led by Ken Mitchell. I took to heart Ken's words that a writer's duty is to entertain. Many of the people I met that first year are still my friends.

Meanwhile the kids grew up and went about their lives, and after eighteen years our marriage broke down. There was blame on both sides but I was very sad. We had been through a lot together in over eighteen years.

However, the children grew up and got educated: Odell a sought-after computer programmer; Scott an award winning journalist and writer; Anne a talented artist and ESL teacher; and Leona, good at pretty much everything.

But circumstances and people change, and life goes on. Lyle married again but I did not. I'm grateful that our son, Scott, arranged for us to make our peace and voice our regrets when Lyle was dying.

Two heartbreaking events.

Leona had finally found her true life partner and was living with Dave in the country outside Edmonton. She loved animals and was so happy. She was killed in a car accident September 2, 2000. I had been going to visit her there. We had some problems in our relationship which we wanted to resolve and I was very happy about that.

Odell died on April 10, 2002, of hepatitis C. He left behind his wife, Gina, and two children, Odette and Christopher.

Teddy

Anne was eight or nine when she saw a puppy at the pet store not far from Rutter Crescent. We had talked about getting a dog and so I went with her to see it. It had been adopted. End of story.

Not nearly.

She came home a day or so later and said the black one in the next cage was even nicer. And it probably was as it was a mixed breed and the first had been a purebred. One look and I was hooked, too. We named her Teddy.

Teddy grew up with the kids, sleeping on their beds, swinging at the playground, chasing snowballs, running around everywhere with them sans leash as dogs did then. She was a great little dog. As time went on she rode on Scott's motorcycle. Slept every night on the orange shag rug in the den as we watched TV. We all loved Teddy.

Anne took her grade eleven at the Lutheran Boarding School at Outlook. When we drove her back after one of the school breaks Teddy went along, of course. After a nice afternoon we said goodbye and went home.

That night in the study room which was in the basement Anne said she felt as if she was being watched, or at least something made here glance up at the window. Teddy was looking in at her. Anxiously looking at her, she said. We'd forgotten to take her home.

Teddy spent that week at the school surrounded by kids who loved dogs. I'm not sure she wanted to come home.

One very rainy day at the lake one summer, everyone was bored. Odell was trying to train Teddy to retrieve a rolled-up newspaper. Then the other kids joined in. They could throw that newspaper till they were blue in the face and Teddy wouldn't retrieve it. She just sat with a stubborn look on her face. Like she was above it all.

When the rain didn't let up we decided to go to North Battleford to see a movie, leaving Teddy in the cabin. We went to the movie and then to have something to eat – before Macdonalds et al. because we went to a café for a regular meal and then headed back to the lake.

As soon as we opened the trailer door Teddy went ballistic. She picked up the newspaper and ran to Odell and dropped it in front of him. Then she did it with Leona, then Anne and Scott. She did it over and over again. She was saying *oh please please please don't leave me just because I wouldn't bring you the stupid newspaper. I thought you were never coming back, I'll do it forever.*

It still makes me feel bad. It also shows what a smart dog she was, how lonely and afraid she was, there all by herself. The older I get the more I love animals and feel for them all. Even the not-so-smart ones.

Many years later, on a frigidly cold afternoon in Saskatoon, Teddy and I went over to see Anne and my grandson, Daniel, who was still a toddler. The house she was renting was a long way from my house in the University area. It was getting dark when Teddy wanted out to widdle and when we called her she was gone. We looked and looked, calling and calling her until it became clear that she was not coming back. The snow was so deep that winter, piled high all along the sidewalks. I drove and drove the streets for hours, the window open at -35, calling and crying, and finally had to give up. At home the radio gave the temperature as going to -40 overnight, a record. I never slept.

It was just getting light in the morning when I heard a bark. It sounded like her but of course it could not be. I ran to the door and there she was. I'll never forget the sight of that black, snowy, little dog. Alive. I think we both cried.

I rubbed her dry, wrapped her up and hugged her till she was warm. She asked to get down on the floor at the foot of the bed and went to sleep. Throughout the day I kept touching her, her heart felt strong, her nose was cold but her feet were hot, a sign of frostbite, I feared. Oh God, was she going to lose her feet? The vet on the phone said that was unlikely since she'd obviously been walking all night. All night long, hour after freezing hour, between those tall snowbanks, she had padded home.

She slept almost twenty hours. I think we both did.

Going to the vet next day, she sat up looking out the window like a tourist, and even seemed to enjoy the wait at his office. He examined her everywhere, her feet were just warm now, her eyes bright, she wagged her tail when he talked to her and she was smiling. Dogs smile, of course they do. It took me longer than she did to get over her adventure.

It was a delight to see the new lease on life this big adventure had given Teddy. She had seemed a bit down, low energy. Now she was a puppy again, or she thought so. It was in the way she ran, bounding around like a dog half her age, her eyes bright, the way she shook something she'd picked up so energetically, her loud barks. Teddy was a new dog.

One last Teddy story.

Newly on my own, I had to go out to the lake and close things up for the winter. The whole beach was deserted. I was glad I'd taken Teddy. I didn't get finished and we had to stay over. I wasn't happy to, since there hadn't been a sign of life all day. Only one car went by on the lake road. We were definitely there alone.

I was in bed reading about 10:30 when I heard footsteps crossing the large cement patio outside the trailer door. Teddy, outside for her last widdle, started barking furiously. I turned off the light. More footsteps and the sound of someone pushing through the bushes close to my window. And then stopping. Teddy was barking frantically now. Terrified, I crept out of bed and tiptoed to the window.

I had – thankfully – locked the door when Teddy went out. I shook so hard I could hardly pull the side of the blind open just a bit and peer out. Just trees and shrubs in the faint moonlight.

The blind shot up.

What kept me from screaming and advertising a woman inside I'll never know, unless it's impossible to scream and have a heart attack at the same time. But I can tell you when you are really terrified, every hair on your body stands up. And I mean every one.

After a while, a long while, Teddy stopped barking and asked to come in. Teddy, as fiercely protective as a wolfhound, saved the day. Or the night. And maybe me.

I was still a wreck the next day, jumping and screaming at any unexpected sound, and we got away at lightning speed. I didn't pack the car, I threw things at it. What didn't get done could wait.

Teddy slept all the way home.

Anne Szumigalski

I met Anne Szumigalski at a meeting of the Saska-tooon Writers' Club, my first timid foray into the writing world. There were about ten people there, from a teenager to seniors, a mixture of men and women. Lots of friendly chatter and laughter. All of these people wanted to write, too.

Sitting next to me was a large woman with long braids and an English accent. She introduced herself and asked me where my interests in writing lay. I thought short stories. I liked her immediately. He name was Anne Shumasomething and we chatted until a large woman called Sally Clubb – who else could be the president? – called the Writers' Club to order.

They had a problem, a serious problem. The treasurer was absent since he had run off with the Club's funds. Never to be seen again, they feared. Mrs. Clubb felt in some way she should have been able to prevent it, and was assured otherwise. Mrs. Clubb battling the bandit flitted through my head.

The discussion went on for some time – had no one seen the perpetrator? Where he had gone and why? Was he in some trouble? Had he run off with a woman? And how would we pay the rent for the month? A new treasurer was confirmed by a show of hands. This problem took up all of the meeting, I don't remember any talk about writing, but knew I'd be back. Wallets came out to deposit in the treasury, we all donated, and Mrs. Clubb would talk to the building owner about the rent.

After the meeting I offered Anne with the braids a ride home and was glad she accepted. I can't remember what we talked about except for two things. I asked her how much money the treasurer had absconded with and she said something like fifty-nine dollars and thirty nine cents, and she laughed, a wonderful laugh that jiggled her whole body. I said he wouldn't get far and we laughed some more.

We talked about family and I told her that I'd forgotten three-year-old Scott at the hairdresser's the day before, I hadn't told anyone else. About racing back with my heart in my mouth.

Oh, I know, it's terrible, she said. I left a new baby in the carriage in front of a London department store and remembered when I was on the train going home. She talked about the desperation of the trip back. The baby was still there, she said. It was a strange experience to bond over but I felt relieved to know that I was not a terrible mother. Or at least not the only one.

It's all about habit, we agreed. I had never taken Scott to the hairdresser's before and she had never taken a baby to town before. By the time we got to her house I had fallen in love with Anne Szumigalski.

When I let her off at her house she invited me to her Poetry Night, held once a month. I accepted the invitation. Not without trepidation. I hadn't written a poem since high school. Just come, she said, you don't have to bring a poem.

I worried about it for a week. To walk into a room full of strangers. Talented, educated strangers, I was sure. Nor was adult poetry what I yearned to write, but she had asked me. Maybe I already knew how important Anne Szumagalski would be in my life.

Number 9 Connaught Place. The curved street around the house full of cars, all poets I was sure, but some homeowners probably. I parked around the corner on Idylwyld Drive, though it may still have been Avenue A then.

The wartime house was warmly lit and had a welcoming air. People who know me now don't believe I was ever shy but it's true, and it was with a deep breath that I rang the bell.

A pretty young woman answered the door. Are you Lois? Anne's in the kitchen, come on in, I'm Jean, she said, as she took my coat. The small sitting room was packed. There were people on the couch, on chairs, footstools, but mostly on the floor. I say packed but probably about ten people, maybe twelve. Anne introduced me to everyone and got me a painted wooden chair with a beautiful woven throw on the back.

I sat down and looked around. It was a cozy room with an aquarium on a wide bookshelf where fish darted happily like they were in a party mood. Large windows behind the couch looked out at softly falling snow, lit by windows across the street.

People on the floor were having an amicable argument and laughing. Everyone was drinking wine. Talk and laughter everywhere. Anne said she was glad I'd come and asked if I'd like a glass of wine. Oh oh. I should have anticipated that. I just said I'd have whatever else she had. Ginger ale maybe? Yes, she had that. I had drunk so much ginger ale since stopping drinking I was sick of it but gladly welcomed a glass in my hand.

All of these people were younger than I was, late teens, twenties, maybe the smiling, handsome Indian man was older. And the couple, Terry and Caroline Heath, probably in their early thirties. The women intrigued me. The long beautiful hair, short skirts, the long black stockings, the wine glasses, sitting on the floor, I had landed in a bohemian scene.

There were men, smart-looking university guys, and a couple who looked like workmen. And me, a boring housewife with short streaked hair who didn't write poetry. Some people went out for a smoke and I wanted to go, too. I'd quit but still missed that comfort at stressful times.

The door opened and a tall old man in a tweed coat with snow on the wide shoulders came in, followed by a small woman also in a large tweed coat, who took a seat in a corner and huddled in the coat all evening. The man was Alf Bye, warmly greeted by the others. He had driven all the way from Swift Current to attend. At first he looked a bit out of place in that gathering but I soon realized he was not. He was a man who loved poetry and that was all you needed to belong. I never heard the wife's name.

After a while Anne asked who had something to read, and the real purpose of the gathering started. I was by no means a poet and never would be, but was struck by how good these poems were. By an original simile, a powerful image – the moon rode the rails to the nearest town – emotion, rhythm. Alf Bye stood up to stentoriously read a long poem full of passion, rhyming, and I thought of Uncle Jim reciting at the farm. Taken with Alf's size and obvious love of words,

I couldn't have said what the poem was about when he sat down. That happened every time Alf read at poetry nights.

Yes, I went back, attracted to the people and their love of words. I would try to write a poem. And I'd begun to realize the depth of Anne's understanding of poetry, and her generosity in trying to make others' work as good as it could be. I didn't know then that she was already an internationally acclaimed poet.

A funny story about Alf Bye. I had realized that Alf was in love with Anne, perhaps the reason he would drive all the way from Swift Current for poetry nights. Anne and I were talking about Alf one day and she said Oh, I don't know what to do with Alf. He's always kissing me in the most embarrassing places. This was interesting. Where? Where? I asked, eyeing Anne's bountiful bosom. Oh, she said, right out on 2nd Avenue or anywhere.

The names I remember from that poetry night were Terry and Caroline Heath, Jean Okkerse, Mark Abley, Pad (Doctor Padmanab), Bill Ferniuk, Nancy Senior, Eleanor Pearson and Judy Smith.

I kept going for over a year but my poems were totally forgettable except one about running down to the elevator full of self-importance to tell my American father that FDR had died. Seeing him cry.

It was a lucky day for me, and all aspiring writers in the province, when we met Anne Szumigalski. Her enthusiasm, encyclopedic knowledge, generosity and encouragement, and her wonderful laugh will be with me forever.

Victoria

One of the trips we'd all made when the kids were still kids was to Victoria, partly to visit Betty's family. We went on the train, which was fun, until the kids got stomach flu, that is. Leona was the sickest, gushing up from the top bunk. The porter and I dealt with pukey sheets from the bunks several times. I think I saw a black man pale.

Fortunately all recovered in time for the trip on the ferry. The cry of gulls, the exhilarating ocean wind, the passing scenery, all new and exciting.

After a family visit we drove up the Island Highway to Parksville, a lovely little place on the water. The kids and their dad had a great time wading and looking at all kinds of sea creatures. I became an instant beachcomber, excited about the exquisite drift glass, the stones. Each a piece of art, by that mother of all artists.

How good it might be for the soul to be a beachcomber for a year, or part of a year, no worries about kids' problems, no responsibility. A little house close to the water, a dog and a cat and books, waking to the sound of gulls and water. Like the Yeats poem about the little lake house *of clay and wattles made*... I had to look up wattles – material for building fences or walls, consisting of rods interlaced with twigs or branches.

The Lake Isle of Innnisfree – I remember bits – *Nine bean rows will I have there, a hive for the honey-bee,* and these... *And I will have some peace there, for peace comes dropping slow...*

And, the longing voice tells us, in the noisy city, wherever he is, *I hear lake water lapping with low sounds by the shore. I hear it in the deep heart's core.*

To have written lines like these. And, oddly, the only poem I loved in a small Yeats collection. And as for living as a beachcomber with no one to talk to, I wouldn't last more than a few days.

I like the small places up-island from Victoria very much. I'm ambivalent about Victoria. To someone used to the prairie landscape it feels excessive, a beautiful woman wearing too much jewelry. Natural beauty doesn't need so much adornment.

On the other hand, it has beaches to comb. I checked a suitcase the ticket agent could hardly lift. What have you got in there? Stones, I said. Don't you have any stones in Saskatchewan?

I would move to Victoria some time later to help out with my mother, who had moved there a few years before. Betty had a husband and five children, and was constantly aware of Mom being alone. Poor Betty was born guilty. Her sister, too.

After actually moving there I became much more aware that we were on an island – that the people and the places I loved would be, eventually, unbearably far away.

All that water.

And, dare I say, people who live there awhile tend to become insular.

I lived in Victoria for less than a year, having felt it was a mistake while the moving van was still on the ferry. All my friends, the writing community, my sweet house on Osler Street someone else's now. I was homesick. Sometimes you don't know what you have until you don't have it any more. I went home in 1987 to a job as the Writer in Residence at the Saskatoon Public Library that fall, which was a good thing.

My daughter Anne had also moved to Victoria with her eighteen-month-old son, Daniel, and needed a bit more time before she also moved back. Running back to Saskatoon was a very selfish move on my part all around and I'm sorry I didn't handle that better, didn't stay longer for her sake, and for Daniel, whom I adored. For Mom, and Betty. I'm more than a bit shocked by it now. People who say they don't regret anything in their lives make me envious. I regret plenty.

Anne and I both hated how early night came there. She said not long ago the Victoria light was darkness reflecting off of gloom. I understood that. The dark made night driving difficult, no snow to reflect light, just a river of red blurry tail lights ahead, the windshield wipers on high.

And the rain. I used to love the sound of rain on the roof at home. Waking at night in Victoria the roar of rain felt isolating.

Betty and I loved each other but were never really as close as some sisters. I'd hoped that might happen, but four years age difference in childhood, and her early marriage – at nineteen – didn't encourage the closeness I always wished we had.

And we were so different. I visited my grandparents'

hired man, Harvey, in a nursing home in Elrose. My friend Jim, who lived there, took me to see him. Do you know who this is, he asked Harvey. Yes, he said. And I never saw two sisters so different, Betty always looked so nice and you'd have run around naked if they'd let you.

Betty was conservative in her thinking but she changed, over the years, to a much more liberal view of life. I was proud of her for that. That and our both becoming political junkies helped a lot in the later years. Also, she was very supportive of my writing, and I could depend on her to be there for me when I needed her. I miss her very much. She died after suffering the indignity of dementia for the last few years. She didn't deserve that. No one does.

My mother and I had some good times in Victoria. We liked to go down to the waterfront, where Mom would sit on a bench and watch the boats and kites and people, and I would walk the path above the beach, and then sit down to share a smoke with Mom. We both loved our smokes.

We also liked to just get in the car and go with no destination in mind. One such day we drove up the Island Highway, and stopped whenever we felt like it. I bought a wonderful second-hand Chinese woven rug, a soft aqua with roses on the border. It was huge and was my living room rug for over twenty years. It cost $100.

I said when we left we'll just roam around till we get hungry and then we'll stop somewhere for supper. For some reason breaded veal cutlets kept popping into my mind, over and over during the drive, odd since I never ordered them anywhere and hadn't given them a passing thought since Mom ordered them in the old Gold Leaf Café in North Battleford when we were kids. What? Breaded veal cutlets? What were they?

How did she know about them? I was so impressed. The height of sophistication, my mother.

My stomach was rumbling by the time I saw an inviting restaurant and pulled into the parking lot. Thank goodness, Mom said. I've thought of nothing but breaded veal cutlets since I got in the car.

How do we explain things like that?

One windy night, we drove down to the spit of land at the waterfront where people flew kites. It was cold as well as windy, late fall. We parked there and opened our windows a bit to hear and smell the waves crashing in. I like that kind of ozone high you get then, when you want to pull in air beyond what your lungs will hold.

We were entertained by the sight of hundreds of gulls, hunched down everywhere, all facing the same way. Bunched up like that, their feathers blowing, they all looked totally pissed off. I never knew a bird could look like that. Mad as hell, they were. *We should have gone south. Why do we never go south?*

Of course when I left Saskatoon I'd sold my house at a loss, and bought a house I didn't love because it was close to Mom's apartment building. It was in the Oak Bay area, near Oak Bay Village, where halfway-affordable houses were scarce. When you feel homesick, living in a house that doesn't feel right exacerbates it. I missed Saskatchewan people a lot, how we all talk to each other anywhere and everywhere. Missed friends, hearing the phone ring.

I went to the grocery store one day to pick up some things for Mom. Two elderly women were discussing the new large strawberries. Were they as good as the smaller ones? They didn't look right? Should they buy them or not?

They're very good, I told them. I'm going to buy some more.

They turned in my direction, looked me up and down and then turned away without a word. I'd apparently failed some test.

Walking to Mom's Oak Bay apartment, I stopped at the light beside another old woman. The corner across, a pile of dirt for some time, was covered in grass with white stones spelling out "OAK BAY."

That's an improvement, eh? I said to her.

She turned. Looked me up and down, and hurried across on the green light. Maybe it was the eh? that did it. Come to think of it, maybe it's a prairie expression, eh?

And I once joined a lineup at an ATM for some cash. I think now this might have been on a later trip. The lineup moved slowly. No one said a word. One by one those in line reached the bank machine and walked back past the lineup. The machine wasn't working and not one of them had said don't bother, it's broken.

Now in Saskatchewan that would never have happened. Someone in the lineup would have exchanged a few words with the person next in line as we waited. Two or three, people, likely. And the first person to find the machine not working would have let the others know and that would have been good for five minutes of complaining about the bloody banks, and the weather, and maybe whatever the government was doing, good or bad, and we'd all go home feeling better. I have always said that small talk is important:

...The woman in the next cubicle in women's-wear asking which looks better on her, the green or the grey, and does the pattern exaggerate her large bosom. I'd take the green, the woman in the adjacent cubicle says, it brings out the colour of your eyes, and no worries about the bosom. You look good in it.

Nice talking to you.

...And the woman sitting beside you on the bus says she never liked that building with the slitty windows by the library, that it looks like a jail, and you agree it does and you talk about buildings you like or don't like till one of you gets off the bus.

Nice talking to you.

...The farmer in the Co-op store at the second-hand book and magazine exchange, tells you the joke he read in a magazine at the doctor's office once and it's the funniest joke you ever heard. And I'm going to share it before this book is finished.

Nice talking to you.

Little things like that.

Mom understood when I told her how I missed Saskatchewan people. She did, too. And Betty, who was shy, still missed prairie people and I don't think she ever felt really at home in that upscale neighbourhood in Victoria. No talking over the fences there, and if you thought on a fine windy day it would be nice to hang out the sheets it wasn't allowed. My brother-in-law did well in business, and they had a beautiful home. Betty could have had anything she wanted, but she didn't want much.

Something that happened at Mom's building in Victoria reminded me what a broad-minded woman she was.

We were just coming in with groceries, followed by two middle-aged men. Let us help you with that, Mrs. Binns, chatting with her up the elevator and down the hall.

Putting the groceries away Mom said, You know, I think those two men are what they call gay. And they are the nicest people in the place. And when my unmarried daughter was pregnant she worried about telling her grandma. I think that's wonderful, Mom said.

I have to go home, I told Mom the day of the

strawberries. I felt like such a rat – and I deserved to – but wasn't ever going to be happy there. I missed the writing community back home. There didn't seem to be one in BC, or maybe I wasn't there long enough to find it. People said I would make friends. Probably true, but I had these perfectly good friends back home, hardly even used in a manner of speaking. And I wasn't writing.

Being offered the Writer in Residence job at the Public Library in Saskatoon as soon as I came back was good. I was in the right place again.

I told Mom she could come and live with me, and a few years later, she did. I wish she had come sooner, but we had two years and we got closer than we'd ever been. Watching *Pride and Prejudice* on PBS, both of us in love with Mister Darcy. Mom sitting in a chair outside watching me put in the plants. Making oatmeal porridge for her every morning and when it was ready I'd call, It's on the post. My grandfather always cooled his porridge a bit on a post outside the kitchen. I'd knit as we watched TV, holding up the scarf every so often, Is it long enough? I never seemed to know. For a giraffe, she'd say.

I didn't smoke any more, or drink, but allowed Mom to smoke, and poured her a rye and coke before supper every day. I hid her cigarettes once when I went out after she burned a hole in the hardwood floor, and felt horrible when I came home and she was crying because I'd hidden them. I never hid them again.

Not too long before she left Victoria she had cataract surgery. I called to ask what it was like to see so well again. Am I ever wrinkled! was the answer. Everybody's wrinkled! I've been through the same humbling experience.

Mom was not a fan of my adult writing, friends telling her my first novel was 'dirty', embarrassing for her, I'm sure. A problem many writers face. Once when a writer friend asked what he should do, there was a poem in his book being launched about his father that would not please him. It was when Salman Rushdie was in hiding and I said See if Salman Rushdie has an extra bed.

Shortly after Mom came to stay with me, when I hadn't quite sorted out the bed/office situation, I slept on a cot in the dining room. One night I woke up after midnight with a light from the living room. Mom was there reading my book, *The Secret Lives of Sgt. John Wilson.*

What are you doing, Mom, it's late. My mother, who never swore, said, I'm reading this damn book and I can't put it down. I can't tell you how happy that made me.

Well, actually, I lied, she did swear sometimes under duress. Like the time we were taking Teddy home from the veterinarian's. Teddy looked like she was going to throw up, and nervous Mom opened her purse to get a cigarette and Teddy threw up in it. I think she swore at me because I couldn't stop laughing. I bought her another purse.

In the summer Mom liked to sit on a chair on the front steps and smoke. Anne said she liked to see Mom there when she drove up.

I wasn't perfect, but it didn't feel like a burden. I finally had my mother to myself, what I had so wanted when I was a child.

Once I was out with the Old Bags for dinner and didn't feel right. Mom had looked tired when I left and I went home to see if she was all right. I helped her get undressed and ready for bed. I asked if there was anything else she needed and she said, Just keep on taking care of me the way you do, it's absolutely wonderful. I want to cry when I write that. She was so easy to please and God knows I didn't keep house the way she would, and I wish I'd cooked better meals but she never complained.

One Sunday I went all out with a roast and all the trimmings, and a pie. Mom was having a nap in her room next to the kitchen. Did you have a good sleep, I asked when everything was ready. Are you kidding, I thought there were six Chinese cooks in the kitchen. I have been told I'm a noisy cook.

Mom and I went for drives, not often enough, I think now. Our favorite spot in Saskatoon was Diefenbaker Park by the river. I'd park the car with a view of the river and the railroad, there was often a long train while we were there, and I would walk the path that circled the park at least twice. There is a large hill we drove up for a different view. Once the fair was on and we could see the ferris wheel and some other insane thing that shot people with a death wish up and down, screaming bloody murder.

We enjoyed those little excursions. I still miss my mother every day, and am so glad we had that time together.

Finding a Family

I got lost twice driving to Fort Qu'Appelle that first trip in 1971, probably because I was so nervous about attending the Summer School of the Arts, and it was a long, unfamiliar drive. I was going to be spending two weeks with real writers, all strangers, all brilliant, I was sure. And probably all drinkers. I almost turned around and went home but knew I'd hate myself for missing this opportunity.

I arrived at the school, commonly called Fort San, an abandoned tuberculosis hospital or sanatorium, with several large buildings joined by boardwalks. Most were obviously once TB wards. I heard music coming from somewhere and a bagpiper up on a hill. Finding my way to the writers' building, which was empty, I wondered if I was in fact early. Or late for something everyone else knew about.

I noticed a fridge on the stair landing and, clutching my small ginger ale bottle, gone warm in the car, I opened the fridge. It was full to bursting with beer, wine and hard stuff. Evidently the writers had arrived. God. I was six months sober.

I sat down in the lounge and waited.

After a while a lanky guy wandered in and slumped on the couch opposite. He wore a white hat with red polka dots. He looked a wreck. I detected a hangover.

I've just been out with a witch, he said.

Oh?

This was interesting.

She read my aura.

Even more interesting.

What did she say about it?

She said it was full of holes. His name was Reg Silvester.

The wombat will give you a room, he said.

It was as if he'd said the zebra will give you your room. Or the gorilla. I couldn't think of anything to say to that.

A short time later the wombat arrived, in the person of Pat Krause, a woman about my age, with a great husky voice and a great laugh I would hear often over the years. I learned that the "Wombat" – named in honour of W.O. Mitchell – was chosen each year to be the writers' go-to person. I felt better after meeting Pat. And in a strange way, the holes in Reg's aura also made me feel more comfortable. He told me he was in Ken Mitchell's class, too.

Next morning the group met in a small schoolhouse up a hill, where children of the hospital staff had attended when Fort San was a hospital. I was glad to see Reg's friendly face. His aura looked much better.

There were seven of us. Two women about my age. Good. Three people working on novels, which really impressed me. In that first class Ken Mitchell said, The first duty of a writer is to entertain, and I never forgot that.

Our first assignment was to write a story and hand it in the next day. I panicked. Every creative brain cell shriveled up and died. The stories I'd written had evolved slowly. It was midnight when I put together a few pages of something, happily forgotten.

It was a wonderful, difficult two weeks. When offered a drink I said, No thanks, I tend to get drunk and disorderly, which seemed to amuse them, and I got through it somehow.

Ken was a wonderful, encouraging instructor with a great laugh. It didn't take much to make me happy. Just his comments in the margins of a story – 'good', 'great character', 'this is funny' – made me hug myself like a kid. The dream of a lifetime was going to come true. I had lots to learn but was going to be a writer.

My sense of humour, which had abandoned me, returned, and I made friends.

I went there scared and unsure and went home happy, excited and full of plans for the future. I had found a family I didn't know I had.

Students and instructors at Fort San Summer School. Great times.

Going On

By the time Lyle and I broke up we were living in a large bungalow on St. Henry Avenue, across from the river. I rented a suite two blocks away on the same street, which was not smart, since I was so conscious of the house down the street, and had taken another route when driving to avoid it. I was forty-four, depressed and lonely.

Lyle had a reputation as an excellent real estate agent. My only identity was as a wife and mother. I felt adrift in the world. Maybe a lot of divorced women feel this way, whether or not they wanted to be on their own. My first divorce – from Jack – had been a necessity. I know without a doubt I wouldn't have survived in that marriage. But this one really hurt.

Renting a duplex for a couple of years in a different part of town helped.

My first publication, *Ghost House*, a chapbook of stories and poems, came out with Coteau Books in 1976, the year of the marriage breakdown. It was Coteau's second season as publishers, the cooperative brain-child of Geoffrey Ursell, Barbara Sapergia, Bob Currie and Gary Hyland. Coteau Books has done so in-credibly much for the establishment of Saskatchewan writers, and is still thriving.

"A Shortage of Mourners," a story in *Ghost House*, won a Saskatchewan Writers Guild prize. The story is based on something that happened to my friend, Alice Carpenter, who went to the wrong funeral. It was for a man she didn't know, with only two mourners, both women. She didn't want to leave considering the situation but couldn't help crying – only two mourners, two *dry-eyed* mourners, it was too sad. She couldn't stop, the two women turning often to look at her. A mistress, they must have thought, and she made her escape before they could ask who she was.

I think it was during the first Women's Year Day, on a bus from Regina, that I wrestled with the decision of whether to tackle a novel. Scary thought. Maybe there'll be a sign, I thought, chickening out. Walking down a Saskatoon street the next day I saw on the sidewalk as I turned a corner, the largest paper clip I had ever seen, then or since. Curses. I had to do it.

I rented a small corner room, unsuitable for office or suite, in the Ross Block downtown for $25 a month and started the novel. It was about a marriage break-down. Write what you know, some say, and I knew that. The life and family were fictional but the feelings were real.

It's daunting, a first novel. I couldn't seem to write the first words, never mind the first page. Terrifying. So wrote about a dinner party I'd thought of, that be-came chapter six and I was then able to go back to page one. And page two and three and...

It's the time commitment and worry that you don't

have enough to write about that's so scary. And how to fix a story that starts to sag in the middle like an old mattress, and other problems. You learn. Writing that novel was a great learning experience for me.

Working in the Ross Block was good, nothing to do but work. A basement AA coffee room run by Earl, an old guy who had lost most of his brain cells somewhere, was a good place to take a break. His answer to most anything you said, was Yes sir, that's quite a thing. Not much help to the occasional troubled person who wanted to know how to stop drinking. But it was a change of scene and the coffee was good. People from nearby offices dropped in for a cup of Earl's.

Earl told me more than once about a woman he knew: he said she got on a bus one day and when she got off she was dead. Yes, sir, that was quite a thing. Had it really happened to someone? Pressed for details, he didn't have any. Just the facts.

One Ross Block tenant I often saw going or coming wore a capacious white canvas cape with a large message on the back – LET ME BE FREE TO KNIT. What was her message to the world besides a polite F-Off? She walked miles every day past the city outskirts collecting wood. Sometimes you could hear her hammering away upstairs.

Making furniture? What? A great character for a story. Was she healing from some tragedy, I wondered, as I heard her struggling back up the stairs with an armful of wood. She wouldn't use the elevator if anyone was around.

And the Ross Block was good because it was close to the library, which I haunted for books on writing. Over time I read almost all the books in that section, and learned bits about technique, writing seamless flashbacks, etc.

I loved the tremendously exciting process of learning to write. One of the problems I hear beginning writers struggle with is developing a voice. When you're in your forties, the voice is you and you've lived a lot and felt a lot. There's a confidence in the work. Perhaps that's why success came quickly.

When I finished the manuscript for *They Shouldn't Make You Promise That*, I gave up the little office. It had served its purpose. The novel was received enthusiastically by the first publisher I submitted to, New American Library, the paperback arm for Macmillan at that time, and came out in 1981 in the US. The editor said I wrote like Steven King, a compliment I hugged to my heart. I love Steven King. I made only $280 and Macmillan apologized and said that while NAL may not have been crooks, they certainly acted like crooks. It was subsequently published by three more publishers. It is still in print.

Ken Mitchell told me when the novel came out that I'd never write anything that close to the bone again. And Ken may be right. *They Shouldn't Make You Promise That* apparently touched a lot of people who said things like, Were you hiding in my closet when you wrote that? And people liked the humour.

People thought the book was about me and my family, which it was not, except for parts of some incidents and family jokes and pets.

I forget which important writer said all writing is autobiographical. In terms of voice I suppose, shaped by life experiences so it probably is to a degree. The husband in the book bore no resemblance whatsoever to Lyle. And the people I wrote about were good, interesting, funny people I wouldn't mind being associated with.

I bought a small house on Osler Street, close to the university area. It was a lovely house with a fireplace, large corner living room windows, and maple hard-wood. The second bedroom was my office, and I would have many happy, productive years there. Except for things like frozen pipes, thawing them with a hair dryer while folded up in impossible places, swearing. I admit I swear.

It was bright and cheerful, that house on Osler Street, and made me feel the same. I loved that house and it loved me back.

Westgate Books

My second favorite job – after CJNB – was with West-gate Books, a second-hand bookstore on the west side of Saskatoon. The perfect job for a newly divorced person with no particular skills.

It was a good-sized store with everything on offer. History, biography, literary criticism, novels, short stories, nonfiction books on every topic under the sun, a whole wall of romance novels, books from every-where, categories for wars, women writers, men writers, filed according to country, and nonfiction, to just give you some idea of the scope. Everything but porn, unless you count the girlie magazines – Bill Ho-loboff, the owner, didn't like it but there was a demand.

The store had large front windows, and along one wall under the windows were the comics, where you had to watch not to fall over kids rivetted by Super-man, Batman and all those other mans. Circular racks held writers' first small publications, short histories of things like the Frank Slide, odds and ends. It was here I met Sergeant John Wilson of the Northwest Mounted Police, who would take over my life for quite a few years. More about him later.

Bill Holoboff was quite a large man with dark hair – maybe early fifties – who loved books but not necessarily people who liked to read them. He was socially awkward with an abrupt manner of speaking which lost him the odd customer but not many. I don't think he overcame an innate shyness in all the years he ran the business. He lived alone with his mother and I used to feel sorry for him when he put on his coat to go home. He'd have lived at the store if he could.

Bill was a very fair boss, paying us well above minimum wage. The staff included Anne Dutnall, a young, good-natured woman who was fun to work with and take smoke breaks with on the sidewalk, and Alison, a very depressed young girl with long black hair who had recently broken up with her boyfriend. She took crying breaks. I think Anne tried to help her. And there was Jim, an American who was hiding from the Vietnam War. I didn't blame him for that, but he had an annoying, know-it-all attitude.

We paid half for trades in good condition, and the romance readers came with shopping bags full. Some would be looking for a particular number in a series – the read-by-numbers-ladies – and they took as many as they traded. And some of them must have taken speed-reading courses because they were back for more in an astonishingly short time. Those women loved to read – historical romances were the favorites – and more power to those writers who actually made a lot of money writing not very long or complex books. And giving a lot of pleasure to so many women, and maybe the odd man. I thought I'd try my hand at it and wrote one story bought by *True Romance*. They paid by the word, which was interesting. But I didn't have the right nature for it. Not romantic enough.

Westgate Books was a great place to work, and I was grateful for it. I was a book lover, adjusting to being alone, and it worked well for me. Some days I think I bought more books than I sold. We must have got a good deal from Bill.

Funny things happened sometimes. A nervous little man in a hat came in one day and happened to tell me that he was going on a trip to Vancouver. His first plane trip. Someone else rang up his purchase, *Fear of Flying* by Erica Jong. Shocking for the time, lots of sex.

Oh my God, I said to Anne when he left, he thinks it's a book about flying. Well, he's in for a surprise, isn't he? she said, and we laughed. I never saw him in the store again. Maybe died of shock.

It reminds me of an English class where we took *Lady Chatterley's Lover*. The prof said that because Lady Chatterley's lover raised pheasants when he wasn't twining violets in Lady Chatterley's pubic hair the book was sent for review to *Field and Stream*. The reviewer dutifully reviewed it, and said that while there was some good information on raising pheasants the reader had to get through a lot of extraneous material to get to it.

Bill Holoboff died quite a few years after I worked there and Anne took the business over. She was a natural. She moved Westgate Books to the east side and I'm glad she didn't change the name or phone number. When Anne retired Gene Suignard took over the store.

It had to be moved once more. It's in a mall on Louise Avenue just off 8th Street, across from Gibsons Fish & Chips, and there's no better place to browse to your heart's content. It's my favourite place to hang out in Saskatoon and has been since the first time I saw it. I go home with an armful every time, hauling them back for another.

Westgate Books is a wonderful oasis for Saskatoon book lovers and writers. And we love them for it.

Auntie Eva Knitting

It was time for a trip to Turtleford to see my Auntie Eva. Turtleford is about a two-and-a-half-hour drive from Saskatoon. Visiting Auntie Eva was never boring. She was a lifelong Communist – opinionated as ever and didn't care who knew it. I loved that about her. We were not blood-related, but I was closer to her than to any of my real aunts. She and Uncle Askan had lived with us in Mervin when their house burned down.

On the trip to Turtleford, I was thinking about writing another novel. It was the smart thing to do after the success of *They Shouldn't Make You Promise That* but it didn't feel like the right reason to write a novel. And no great story was begging to be written.

When I walked into Auntie Eva's living room, she was actually sitting down. She must have sat down sometimes but I don't remember her that way. She was always on the move, gardening, or cooking or baking and talking, talking, talking. She was a wonderful cook – the supper she'd have ready for me was worth the trip alone. And even in her nineties I had to run to keep up with her. She would become almost totally blind later and her sight was failing fast. When she hauled out the pressure cooker I wanted to hide.

She was knitting something that looked a bit like a long, narrow airport windsock. I knew her daughter Linda was expecting a baby and wondered if that had brought on this unusual activity.

I should say that Auntie Eva was an artist with an embroidery needle and her beautiful pieces, along with her prize gladioli, never failed to win first prize at the Turtleford fair. She was passionate about flowers and embroidery.

Auntie Eva was an atheist and I once asked if she would embroider a Serenity Prayer with flowers for me and was told in no uncertain terms that she wasn't going to be embroidering any blanketyblank prayer. And I should know better than to ask. If I wanted "something sensible" with birds or flowers or both she'd be glad to do that.

She made one of my most treasured possessions, a wonderful grey cat whose enormous eyes peer out through a mass of flowers. It's done in very light wool and the cat's eyes are rivetting. I'm so glad she wouldn't countenance the blanketyblank prayer.

What are you knitting? I asked.

She held it up and looked at it.

It's a hat for Linda's baby, she said. She thought for a moment. And if the baby fits that hat I hope they kill it.

That was Auntie Eva.

All the way home I was stopping the car to write Auntie poems. Auntie had become a knitting-challenged expectant mother:

Auntie's knitting a baby bonnet
That looks like the lid of a pot;
If Auntie's baby fits that hat
It's not going to look so hot.

Auntie's knitting a baby bonnet
That looks like a hot air balloon;
When they tie that hat on the baby
It'll float right up to the moon.

Auntie's knitting the baby a suit
With a maple leaf all white and red;
If they don't have a flag on Canada Day,
They can fly the baby instead.

By the time I got home I had the spine for a collection of children's poems.

Novel be damned. I had fallen in love again.

Bowled Over by Poems

My love of rhyming poetry had erupted like a big, colourful fish leaping out of a pond singing, Look at Me! Look at me!

I was a goner.

I loved loved loved writing poems for kids. Who knew? It was like being eight years old again. I saw poems everywhere. Anywhere. A ladybug on my bathroom window became

Bug

On the window in the washroom
At our school yesterday,
A little bug was crawling in
Its little buggy way.
I whispered in its tiny ear
To not make any noise;
Because it was a ladybug
And the washroom is for boys.

I laughed when I wrote that, and thought of Ken Mitchell's advice about a writer's duty to entertain. In the months ahead I would entertain myself banging away on a typewriter in my office on Osler Street, re-writing pages over and over or dabbing mistakes with White Out. Scott, a university student then, was staying with me. He said Mom, for heaven's sake get a computer. I got an IBM Selectric, God's gift to writers, instead, and that helped a lot. I wasn't ready for a computer yet.

When I finally was, I took a computer lesson in a computer store downtown. That experience almost turned me off at the outset. Anne called to say, How was the computer lesson?

Terrible, I said. I spent a whole day shut up in a windowless room next to a fat man called Lloyd who kept hitting me. (He had slapped my hand every time I reached for the wrong key).

Poems and poems and poems, reaching for the yellow legal pad by my bed every morning. Drinking coffee and writing funny poems. It was wonderful.

A black humour appeared in quite of few of them.

Lonely

I'm a lonely boa constrictor,
I'm as sad as the saddest sack;
I keep hugging people all the time,
But nobody hugs me back.

Fred

My mother gave me a little plant
That was nearly almost dead,

222

I made up my mind to save it
And I named it Little Fred.

I fertilized and watered Fred
And talked to him a lot;
Hi Fred! Whatcha doin' Fred?
Looks like it's going to be hot.

And Fred just sat in his little pot
On my bedroom windowsill,
Soakin' up sunshine and water and words,
Cookin' up chlorophyll.

Then one day he started to grow,
He shot out all over the place;
He grew out of bigger and bigger pots,
He grew at a terrible pace.

He grew till he filled up the window
He grew till he filled up the room,
Till he covered the dresser and closet and bed
In a sinister greeny gloom.

After I moved to another room
We heard rustling noises in there,
And sometimes munchy and crunchy sounds.
I think Fred devoured my chair.
Dad said he wasn't scared of a plant
As he marched right through the door;
Fred rustled and munched and burped a bit,
Now Dad's not here any more.

Mom is feeling really annoyed,
She says it's an awful bother;
Nobody wants to buy a house
With a room that eats up fathers.

Now Fred is starting to push his leafy
fingers around the door;
We're packing as fast as we possibly can
And moving to Singapore.

A lot of creatures found their way in, too.

Hi!
I'm a trapdoor spider
I'm waiting down here
For some unsuspecting creature;
Then I'll kill it and tear it
Limb from limb,
It's my least attractive feature.

You get the idea.

I recently read in the paper about a scientist whose
trapdoor spider died at the age of forty-one. It upset
him. He had hoped it would make it to fifty. I imagine
him in his lab praising her, Good Girl! every time she
popped out and trapped something.

I remembered this eight-year-old feeling:

Just Because...

Just riding my bike
With the wind in my hair,
Not really going...
...Anywhere.

Not doing a thing
That I know I should;
Just riding my bike
'Cause it feels so good.

And not so great times kids go through. "Horrible Morning" is about getting ready to go to school on a January morning, with homework not done. Your baby brother is just playing in his snuggy pyjamas, and the cat's curled up on your bed, all furry and purry and fat. And you want to be the baby brother. You want to be the cat.

And you sometimes feel jealous:

Bonnie

Bonnie's pretty. Bonnie's smart,
Bonnie has a horse;
Her bike is new, her doll is, too,
The newest one, of course.

Her brother's cute and not a brute,
They've been to Disneyland. Twice!
Oh, why do I have to know *Bonnie*?
Oh, why does she have to be *nice*?

A dreaded arithmetic test became "Arithmetic Test" – this poem would be very often recited by classes at oratory competitions, still is. It came straight out of my childhood after missing months of school with rheumatic fever and being put ahead in school.

Just one more? About Scott's wandering turtle. Kids love it.

Wanderlust

Oh, no! We're missing Edgar again,
It always gives us a scare;
That fat old turtle with squashy feet
Has vanished into the air.

He's going to catch his death of cold
With his head all bony and bald;
Oh where, oh where has our Edgar gone,
Now where had that turtle crawled?

Is he in the petunias? Under the stoop?
Simmering softly in turtle soup?
Is he under the fridge or in the oven?
Gone to McDonalds for Egg Mcmuffin?

Is he off to the monster matinee?
Shopping for suits at the Hudson Bay?
Is he robbing a pet food store? Or a bank?
Oh, here he is, sleeping behind his tank.

We have to keep watching Edgar these days,
He's becoming addicted to travel,
 He's tired of nibbling lettuce leaves
And standing around in the gravel.

Anne Simmie's illustration shows Edward hitchhiking with a sign, "TURTLEFORD OR BUST!" Good children's illustrators add a new dimension to the text.

When the collection was almost finished I rented a charming little suite in Victoria. I had the pleasure that winter of looking at an original portrait by Group of Seven artist Frederick Varley. He was a relative of the suite's owner, who, like many Victorians, was heading south until spring. I made friends with a retired newspaperman who liked to do the same things I did – going to book stores, walking by the ocean. Talking. Spending time with Mom and Betty. I became an addicted beachcomber.

I wrote the final poems there. Titled the manuscript *Auntie's Knitting a Baby* and submitted it to Western Producer Prairie Books in Saskatoon. And received a prompt and enthusiastic phone call from the editor, Rob Sanders.

I was so excited. My hair went curly.

Auntie's Knitting a Baby came out with Western Producer Prairie Books in 1984. Rob asked for submissions from artists for the illustrations, including Anne's line drawings. Anne had studied at Calgary and Medicine Hat art schools. Rob sent all the submissions to a number of children's picture book authors, including Janet Lunn. The almost unanimous decision was that Anne's drawings best captured the spirit of the poems.

Good reviews came in. And the most fun was yet to come. Reading to kids in schools far and wide. And getting lost on more roads than I can remember.

My first time reading to kids came when Wayne Dyer, the Saskatoon East School Division superintendent and a very big man, asked me to accompany him to the schools to read poems to the students. I was nervous, but Wayne was the kind of guy who would put anyone at ease.

I remember him sitting on the floor with the kids, telling them a spooky story, the kids laughing so hard they fell over all around him. It was a great thing to see. By the time we returned I was quite comfortable reading to the grade three and four kids.

This was the beginning of the busiest, craziest, funniest, most creative period of my life, with lots more poems to come. The second collection, *An Armadillo*

Is Not a Pillow, was published in 1986, also by Western Producer Prairie Books.

Between the last two collections was a story in rhyme called *What Holds Up the Moon?*, published by Coteau Books. It's a story of a girl asking various people what holds up the moon, and the answer according to what they do: Stitches, said the doctor, the dressmaker, too; Mortar, called a man who was working on a wall; the paperhanger told her it was glue. And so on. Anne's coloured pencil illustrations are quite lovely and fun, and teachers told me they would show kids the pictures to inspire them to work with coloured pencil.

Who Greased the Shoelaces?, the third book of poems, came out in 1989 with Stoddart Publishing. I think by then Rob had moved to work for Douglas and McIntyre in Vancouver.

Writing my other children's books gave me just as much pleasure as the first one.

All of them were gifts, and I'm grateful.

You Can't Miss It.
Cows.

A problem I've had all my life reared its inconvenient head when the poetry books came out and with them requests to come and read in schools all over the place. I have no sense of direction, and once got lost in the old Hudson Bay Store in Saskatoon. On the road it might have something to do with not paying attention at the right time.

We'd love to have you, they said. I'm a sucker for that, throwing caution to the winds. Someplace I'd never heard of? No problem. I always asked and accepted for grades three and four. So far so good.

People think it's funny, but having no sense of direction can be enormously stressful, as all directionally challenged people know. Especially when you're driving to places you've never been and when it's taking longer than they said it would, you automatically think you're lost. It's called conditioning, I think, brought on by the many times you've been there. Well, somewhere. And unless the sun is rising or setting you don't know west from south or wherever.

Anxiety sets in. Did you somehow get on the wrong road? Miss the one into the town? Should you keep going hoping the town will appear around that long bend up there or should you flag down the next vehicle and ask for directions? Usually a farm truck. Most often it was the right road and you could put that nagging fear away and enjoy the scenery. Until it seems to take longer than the truck driver said. Had you heard him right? Are you sure?

But I do listen a bit more carefully to the person I stop on a country road, unlike the many times on foot in an unfamiliar place, say Glasgow, or North Battleford, or a small prairie town where you can't find the school. While the stranger gives me directions I'm thinking what beautiful eyes and long eyelashes this girl has, or what a handsome old man he is, or how sad that boy looks, and I still don't know how to get where I'm trying to go. And people who do know the way sometimes forget a small detail in giving directions.

One such time stands out. I was doing readings at two schools, in two different towns, in one day. I can't remember the names of the towns. If I'd ever thought of writing a memoir I'd have kept a journal. The names of many of those places are lost. But not the experiences, if stressful.

Arriving at a school always felt good. I felt at home in schools and on entering a new one asked the first kid I saw to direct me to the staff room. Even the littlest kid knew where it was. I'd hang up my coat, help myself to coffee if there was some, and wait for the teacher. She – most times a woman – would take me to the library and bring me a small table to sit on while reading, and to put books, water and, hopefully, coffee on as well. I could see the kids so much better from a table. I loved these women. They were wonderful.

I had fun with the grade threes and fours, enjoyed a very good lunch and visit with the teachers and it was time to set off for the next school. Detailed instructions were supplied.

After you go down the very long hill and you see the feedlot on your right, you take the *first* road left. The first road, they stressed that, I remember it clearly. *The first road, you can't miss it*, they said, waving goodbye at the school door. I had already asked which way to turn out of the teacher's parking lot or wherever my car was, how to get out of town and aimed onto the road to the next. I asked these things every time, asked them to draw a map sometimes, or I could end up seeing signs for the wrong town suddenly blooming along the highway. I hated that.

Setting off, it was a nice fall day, I remember, and these trips could be very enjoyable, especially in the fall when the country was luscious with colour. And the trip home when I'd done a good job, enjoyed the day and knew where I was going and could relax. But not quite yet.

It wasn't too long before I got to the long hill and they weren't kidding, that hill was really long, and soon after that I spied the feedlot on the right. Big sigh of relief, it's so great when everything goes right.

I slowed down, searching for the first road to the left. And there it was. But this narrow, muddy, rutted road looked like an oxcart track, chewed up by huge tires, so it couldn't be the right road. Could it? But I could hear them stress, the first road to the left. Two or three people said it. I pulled to the side of the road and stopped. Now what to do? I was due at the other school in about half an hour.

While I sat there thinking, the cows in the feed lot sounded excited about something, and when I got out of the car I caught a glimpse of something that looked like a red shirt down at the far end. And a truck around the back.

I crossed over to the rail fence and climbed up to see. Thank God, a man in blue jeans and the red shirt feeding the cows down at the other end. He could tell me what to do.

Hello! I yelled, and the cows all turned their heads in my direction and bawled an enthusiastic welcome. MOO! they all said. MOO! So glad to see yoo! You're just in time for lunch! MOO! MOO! I had always liked cows and apparently they liked me, too.

I yelled louder. They mooed louder. Hello! MOO! MOO! Hello! MOO! This went on for some time and the man never looked up. Of course he couldn't hear me.

Leaning farther over in a vain attempt to catch his attention, my glasses fell off into the muddy lot. I'd been meaning to get them tightened but hadn't got around to it. And while I was thinking maybe I could reach them between the lowest rails a cow stepped on them. The man never looked in my direction.

I finally gave up, and tried to drive down the muddy track – *the first road left*, and got stuck about a quarter of a mile along it. Of course, my gleeful inner critic jumped in, Any sensible person would have known it was not the road. Shut up, I said, and got mercifully unstuck after a few nerve-wracking maneuvers. Back on the main road I came to a civilized road left and found my way to my next appointment. Only a little bit late.

Another great bunch of kids who laughed a lot at the poems. What could be better than that. A girl told me her dog had eight puppies and then its husband ran away. Who could blame him? Domesticity was not in his DNA.

Oh, well, I thought, on the highway with the sign that said "SASKATOON," the Writers Guild cheque would almost pay for new glasses and I'd been wanting new frames. Life was good.

Especially when you know where you're going.

Auntie, the Play

It must have been sometime in 1991 that Tom Bentley Fisher, the director of 25th Street Theatre, called me to set up a meeting. About what? He'd tell me when we met.

He wanted me to write a children's play incorporating many of my poems which would be part of the dialogue. I said I would think about it, but was worried about how that would work. It will, Tom said. And he was right.

Writing that play was pure joy from beginning to end. Falling in love with the genre. It happened whatever the genre.

When the script was finished and approved by Tom, I got an unbelievable case of hives, which spread from my head to the back of my knees, huge, insanely itchy hives that wouldn't stop. A skin specialist and lovely man, Doctor Gen, admitted me to hospital, and to three days of constant intravenous prednisone. Doctor Gen was away and another doctor sent me home on the Sunday with no follow-up withdrawal prescription.

The next day the play went into rehearsal and I had trouble concentrating, my mind like a pinball machine. However, it slowly got better and being there for rehearsal was amazing, seeing how the actors owned and expanded their roles so quickly, and how scenes evolved under Tom's director's eye, it was brilliant. Lots of laughs.

Four actors played multiple parts and they were amazing. Sharon Bakker (Jane, Bonnie, Mrs. Semcoe); Ralph Blankenagel (Caleb, Jack, the Dog); James Klaasen (Simon, Albert, the Dog); and Elizbeth McRobbie (Annie, Miss Hassel, the Dog). They didn't so much act like Grade Four kids as become them.

The story starts on the first day of Grade Four and ends on the last. It takes them from home to school, from fall to winter to spring. Kids' joys, kids' problems.

A Cam Fuller review read, *You could have heard a snowflake drop when Blankenagel switched into the role of the bully, Jack, in which he was truly threatening. McRobbie's hilarious imitation of a very self-satisfied Frisbee-catching dog drew spontaneous applause. Bakker's instant switches to Bonny, who is smart and has curly hair and has been to Disneyland twice, were totally convincing... And you didn't know whether to laugh or cry when Klassen became Albert, the class nerd who can't spell.*

I found the first snowfall scene with the two girls lying in the snow beautiful. And a chance to give a word its real meaning. Awesome, they said. Awesome.

Opening night was amazing, the theatre lobby walls decorated by my friend Betty Meyers. The seats were full.

Seeing *Auntie*, the polished product, was an extraordinary experience. Those actors had the audience riveted. And you could tell they were having fun.

Cam Fuller's review ends this way: *What's not to like? While the adults bathed in nostalgia, the kids were transfixed by seeing their own experiences and feelings illustrated before their eyes. This play could tour every elementary school in the country and not run out of steam. Of course, that would deny the country's grown-ups the chance to see it.*

Auntie's Knitting a Baby, the Play, opened December 22, 1992. A surprising, unforgettable experience, from beginning to end.

Mining for Stories

Short stories were my first love, and writing stories of a specific length – eight pages – for the radio program, *Saskatchewan Short Stories*, taught me a lot. You really had to start the story in the first sentence, create interesting characters, develop the story to a climax, and add an ending. Sometimes the main character changed in some way, but not always. You tried to create vivid details. Tell a good story.

After the novel, I started to write short stories without the time constraints of radio. I went back to the most painful, long-lasting experience of my childhood, rheumatic fever. The memories, still vivid, always would be. I forget which important writer said that if you survive childhood you will have enough to write about for the rest of your life.

But now it's a story, right? Important things have to change. The good father becomes a rotter who leaves for good without even saying goodbye while Amy is sick, stuffing his clothes in a bag in the dim bedroom, thinking Amy can't see. Amy has an older sister, I had an older sister. I gave the whole experience to Amy, almost every detail. Miss Bolt reads to her from the Bible. She hears – as I did – Miss Bolt praying out loud on her knees between their beds, Please God, don't let Amy die in the night. The wintergreen rub, the itchy red flannel on her joints. The enema. The feelings. The loneliness. She tolerates it all. What else can she do?

This was all good material and I mined it with a will. Nothing wrong with that. The story is called "Romantic Fever" since we don't know why the father runs away, is it to someone else? And the last scene forecasts a romance for the mother, with someone who'd be a good father.

I wrote that story in third person, present tense, wanting her experiences, all in one room, to feel like they're happening now. I didn't want first person – that is, I feel scared, I hurt all over, etc. – since it would sound whiney. Before we write anything, that combination must be thought about, as it affects the story. The most common combination is third person, she or he, past tense. I chose first person, present tense for my novel, and we only see what Eleanor sees, feel what she feels. This is called the unreliable narrator, since we only know what she's telling us and it may or may not be true.

Something interesting about "Romantic Fever": Lorna Crozier asked if I called the nurse Miss Bolt because she was like a lock on my door. My prisoner. That thought had never crossed my mind, unless it had subconsciously. But it felt right.

The second story in the book is "Red Shoes." About a girl staying at her grandparents' farm while her parents, who were not getting along, were in Kentucky. When they asked what she'd like them to bring her, she said red sandals. They did bring red sandals, but they were both for the same foot. Straight out of my childhood. Another good mining expedition. As soon as I put on my helmet with the light on the front lighting the passages, stories fall out of the cracks. I forget which writer said, All fiction is autobiographical. And I suppose in a way, it is. Perhaps informed by voice, past experiences, and a certain way of looking at the world.

One of the stories called "Pictures" – completely fictional – yes, I can make up whole stories – is about a strange little girl who drew beautiful pictures with blue trees, yellow skies, green birds. Pictures like jewels.

While writing it I dropped in to see Elyse St. George. Elyse was in her studio and a stunning painting on her easel stopped me short. It was a black hound with red eyes and claws lying among full-blown red poppies with blue and black woven stems surrounded by green and pink ferns. Oh, my God, I said. Can I have that on the cover of my short stories? She said, Yes, you can.

The book is called *Pictures* and I have never seen a more beautiful cover. Caroline Heath, friend and Fifth House publisher, had posters done which people loved and framed. Thank you again, Elyse.

Another story, "Emily," comes from my learning to float at the lake taught by a very large woman. In the story the woman becomes a fat girl. Boys hung around, teasing her, and sometimes she went with them into the bushes. I wasn't happy with the story and kept thinking there was something about Emily I didn't know. I woke up one morning with the words in my head: She is deaf and dumb. And innocent. Wanting to be liked. And the story became something else entirely.

At the Arts Board Summer School, Lorna Crozier loved the story and instigated taking students to the lake where we gathered around on the grass by the water and I read the story of Emily, who had become so real to me. We did it several times. In different years. A kind of tradition.

Having been a very observant child has helped me as a writer. Morley Callaghan said, There is only one trait that marks the writer. He is always watching. It's a kind of trick of the mind and he is born with it.

Pictures came out in 1994, the same year as *Auntie's Knitting a Baby.*

Unknowables

I had a very nice relationship in my late forties with Larry Barton, a man from Weyburn I met through my friend, Ella. He was a healer, and a very interesting guy. He once completely healed a baby covered with a painful rash, shocking himself as much as the baby's mother. He studied long-distance healing and had had some success with that. He wore a gold hoop earring I liked.

One summer during my Fort San workshop with Lorna, I got a call from my sister in Victoria. Mom had suffered a very serious heart attack in Turtleford, and the doctor had sent word that we should come.

In a panic I threw my things together. Lorna and Patrick Lane helped me pack, I remember Patrick carefully lining up sanitary napkins in my suitcase. I left Fort Qu'Appelle at night and stopped in Regina to call Larry about Mom, and ask him if he could try to help. In Saskatoon I called the Turtleford hospital to ask if I should keep going, another two-and-a-half-hour drive. They said it would be all right to come in the morning.

Arriving at the hospital before noon I found Mom, smiling in a pink bed jacket. She looked a heck of a lot better than I did. She knew Betty was coming and gave me a list of things to get at the Co-op store so we'd have groceries in the house. I talked to the doctor, who said she'd had a 'massive' heart attack and suffered a lot of heart damage. It did not look good.

Betty arrived the next day and we visited Mom, discussing after visits how she seemed strangely upbeat for someone in her condition. I said if they would let me I'd take Mom home with me for whatever time she had left. The doctor called and arranged a meeting for the next day.

When we sat down across the desk from him he leaned back in his chair and said, Well, your mother is going to be written up in the medical journals. Because a new test has shown her heart damage has completely reversed. There's no doubt about it, and no one can explain it. I got goose bumps.

I told him about Larry but he just shook his head. Who knows, he said. I sure don't.

Larry moved to B.C. a year or so later to work with someone there, someone who could help him improve his ability. We stayed in touch and about a year later, he died. A friend of his called to tell me he'd had a heart attack.

Mom went on to enjoy seventeen more years.

You Can't Miss It.
Cookies.

The most stressful moment in getting lost is the first inkling that it might be happening. Again. Directionally challenged drivers will know that moment.

It comes again on an unfamiliar road from Regina to, hopefully, Fort Qu'Appelle.

This is taking too long, something says. *You should be almost there by now,* and no highway sign that '*There*' is imminent, or even somewhere ahead, has appeared. That blessed sign all getting-lost people want to get out and kiss, is not over the next hill, not around the next bend, not anywhere because once again you didn't listen well enough when you asked directions.

Here I am again, Mister Frost, the road not taken somewhere behind me.

Then the hunt for someone to ask begins. Not as easy on a highway as on a country road, where you can slow down to watch the flock of snow geese feeding in a field, and the driver behind slows down and passes with a wave.

Highway drivers know where they're going and think you should too. They are not as forgiving of that car that slows and pulls over at every possibility: the house that looked promising but is no longer occupied, that driveway heavily lined on both sides by trees so thick they feel like a smug "No Trespassing" sign, *We don't care if you're lost. It's your own damn fault.*

You stop at a small older house, close to the road. From the dead-grass driveway you have a closer look. Ancient paint curling off the walls. A broken front step. Foiled windows. This place is awful, but there's an old black truck parked just ahead so someone is here and you need help.

You knock on the door. Silence. Knock again. Louder silence.

A drawn curtain twitches. The hair on the back of your neck goes up and you suddenly know you don't want to meet whoever is in there. Back on the highway, resolving to only ask at service stations from now on, and you'll write it all down. Or get them to draw a map. Come to think of it, why don't *you* have a map? You'll get one at the first service station. The one where they'll say, oh lady, you've gone sixty miles in the wrong direction. But service stations are scarce on the ground out here. *You have to stop getting lost, it's really, really depressing.*

Finally, oh wonder of wonders, a big, prosperous looking building. "DAD'S COOKIES," it proudly proclaims. A cookie factory! Here in the middle of nowhere, could it be a mirage? It's odd to say the least but there it is. Making cookies and providing them to salesmen or whatever weary traveller needs a cookie.

What could be nicer? Like your mother and grandma are looking out for you.

Cookies mean love. I need a cookie.

I pull in and get out of the car. At the top of the wide steps a heavy door opens onto a large reception area. A large, empty reception area, the huge, modern desk unattended. I wait a few minutes thinking she – or he – has just stepped out. Receptionists are seldom men but all the women are probably in the back baking cookies. Metal saloon doors lead somewhere. When no one appears I finally ring a bell on the desk.

After another few minutes I ring it again, and faintly, as if from far, far away, the sound of footsteps approaching. Female footsteps since the feet are in high heels.

Tap tap tap tap, coming closer, tap tap tap, tap, almost here; the saloon doors fly open and a woman with her hair all piled up on top of her head takes one look at you, says, I'm sorry, we're right out of broken cookies, and she's gone, the doors swinging, her footsteps fading and finally gone.

I'm sorry, we're right out of broken cookies?

The word 'flabbergasted' comes to mind.

I think of ringing the bell again but am positive she'll know it's me, that poor beggar looking for broken cookies.

Back in the car I look in the mirror, thinking somehow I must look like a person in need of broken cookies. Maybe I have my pinched, worried, *shit! I'm lost again* look that could be misconstrued. I look at my long denim skirt, Indian shirt, sandals. Maybe there's a doomsday cult of hippies nearby: they've run out of money and are getting by on broken cookies till the apocalypse. Then they'll turn into zombies, swarm the factory and eat all the cookies, and the cookie dough, and the woman with her hair all piled up, only her high heels left.

But that's just wishful thinking.

I drive back out to the highway. If I just keep on going I'll eventually get someplace.

Wonderful Times

The Saskatchewan writing scene was electric. We all felt a part of something important. Ken Mitchell and Anne Szumigalski, our already-established writers, were the driving force behind the formation of the Saskatchewan Writers Guild. What a gift that was. New ideas came to fruition, like the formation of the Writers' Retreats. First at the location of the Saskatchewan Summer School of the Arts; later at St. Peter's Abbey, a Benedictine monastery in Muenster, just a few miles from Humboldt. Benedictines are known for their hospitality and these monks were great. I remember Lorna Crozier seeking badminton rackets for a game in the gym, and one of the brothers producing them with a flourish from under his robe.

People got more work done in two weeks of steady writing, hung over some days or not, than seemed possible when the world intruded. And hanging out with other writers after work was always lots of laughs.

Between the Arts Board Summer School and the

Writers' Retreats, great times were spent with Lorna Crozier. David Carpenter. Byrna Barclay. Geoffrey Ursell. Barbara Sapergia. Bob Currie. Gary Hyland. Gertrude Story, so many more.

I was comfortable doing school readings and looked forward to them, except for the getting lost part. I loved making the kids laugh and answering questions after. We shared stories about cats and dogs and so much more. Moving, for example. I'd written a poem about missing your home, your friends, and was surprised by the response from kids who'd also moved – some of them two or three times; about eating liver or not, instigating another poem, and one of them always asked how old I was and didn't always get a truthful answer, I told one boy I was ninety-five and he nodded like that's what he'd guessed. I was probably forty-five. They liked the black humour of some of the poems. I took requests.

On a reading tour in B.C. I read to a class of grade three Chinese kids. Black bangs, sweet round faces, so attentive. After every poem I read there was a tinkle of laughter that went on and on, sometimes when the poem wasn't funny. I asked the teacher about it later and she said she'd told them a writer was going to read them funny poems and they were to be sure to show how much they liked them.

Later on that same tour, I read to a class of grade fours. It was spring and I was allergic to a lot of the unfamiliar foliage, constantly sneezing and blowing my nose. At the end of the session, the teacher told them that I would like it if they wanted to write a poem and send it to me. On the way out the door a boy handed me a poem on a piece of creatively folded paper. I stopped to read it.

Today a writer came,
She told us her dog was lame;
Her poems were funny,
But her nose was runny,
Today a writer came.

Wow! I read it out to the other kids and said it was a perfect poem, which it was. It had rhyme and rhythm and told a story, and I hoped he'd keep writing. I don't think he needed that encouragement.

Sometimes, when a whole week of readings were booked at several schools in a district, morning and afternoon usually at each, occasionally three in one day, it was exhausting, especially with an evening adult reading added after two schools.

During one such week at schools in Coronach, near the Saskatchewan-USA border, I was going to an evening library reading. Driving an unfamiliar road in the dark, what I took to be the lights of town turned out to be an enormous vehicle with scattered lights. As it drew near, a deer stepped onto the right shoulder of the road and turned to look at me. I was terrified, sure it would be killed by me or the oncoming behemoth. It didn't move but my heart was still hammering when I got to the library. I needed the money the readings but after the deer so trustingly turned to look at me that night, I turned down requests that involved driving strange roads at night.

On those chock-full programs I always hoped to be put up in a hotel or motel, where I could eat in the diner or in my room and stretch out on the bed with the television and no one to talk to. Staying at a bed and breakfast, writers were expected to be sociable, eating with other people and visiting with the proprietress – always a woman – when coming back exhausted. And with a sometimes-cold room full of frills and a bed that required a ladder to climb into. And once with a cracked toilet seat that pinched my butt. I liked a motel where they didn't give a damn about you unless you got roaring drunk and ran around the halls naked.

They were wonderful times. I loved driving, am a fairly fast driver, but slowed often to take in the scenery, once swans in a field, hard to believe, from where to where I wondered, an interesting village to drive through or stop for a coffee and a tour of the general store, perhaps an antique store, and heading home through light and shadow at that beautiful part of the day.

Going home happy with the way the readings had gone, remembering kids laughing, telling me funny stories, the liver one was pretty funny. Remembering the wonderful, dedicated teachers who always made me feel so welcome. Women you'd like to have for friends. I loved it all.

And because children's writers were thin on the ground then, the requests were many. And the Saskatchewan Writers Guild cheques, $100 a reading to start with, $150 later, and mileage, were needed and appreciated.

Being paid for having a good time is as good as it gets.

The OBC

Women friends are so important, especially as we age. Six of us regularly got together for dinners out, or took turns having dinner at home: Anne Szumigalski, Elyse St. George, Betty Meyers, Lorna Russell, Marlene Zora and me. All artists and writers: Anne Szumigalski, poet; Lorna Russell, beautiful prairie landscape artist who loved the land; Elyse St. George, visionary, breathtaking paintings from a truly singular mind, and later, writer; Betty Meyers, a storyteller writ large in paint in very large, very populated paintings, every face individual, and other, smaller works; Marlene Zora, making beauty with clay; and Lois Simmie, writer of many genres.

We were often looking for different places to write or paint, and one lovely fall day were all at Lorna's house/studio in the town of Alvena, in the country she loved to paint. Betty also had a house studio in Alvena. We got talking about how important our group was to each of us and thought it should have a name.

We decided on the OBC because it sounded important. Respectable. The OBC.

Old Bags Club.

The Old Bags Club loved to eat out, at our special round table on a riser at Earls Restaurant. Catching up. Gabbing. A drink or so, except for yrs trly, and always laughter. Lots and lots of laughter. People loving what they did. Wonderful years.

I can't remember a particular special get-together. They were all special.

We lost Anne, a huge loss. Betty moved back to Victoria, another big loss. The remaining Old Bags and friends meet twice a month in Elyse's Broadway condo for Scrabble. Older but not necessarily wiser. We still argue.

Here's to The Old Bags Club. And friendship. Especially womens'.

Betty Lee and Oliver

After the three books of children's poems, and the story collection, *Pictures*, short stories came calling again and I welcomed it. Writing stories always felt good; each story wandering around in my head for quite a long time, scribbled bits everywhere.

Betty Lee Bonner Lives There, the most awkward title of all time, and which makes no sense at all, came out in 1991. I hope I didn't suggest the title.

The first story "Sweetie Pie," about a hung-over loser called Al and his pet cockatoo on a car trip with a fed-up woman, came after I visited a couple who had a pet cockatoo which flew onto my shoulder when their door opened. They were crazy about that bird which was bigger than their dog.

The story cockatoo could imitate the sound of a toilet flushing, like the pet parrot at the Bay I used to take the kids to see. You're a monkey's uncle from Chicago, it always said, and cackled at the joke, then made the toilet flushing sound. Its cage had hung right by the washroom in the pet store. A perfect imitation.

I wrote "Harvey and the Heavenly Host" in Victoria after watching guys playing soccer in a thick fog. "The Artist" came from seeing dog droppings decorated with flowers in Beacon Hill Park. "Going Around" was about a woman shopping with a ferocious hangover, and is quite funny if I do say so myself.

And there were serious stories, too. "I'll Take You Home Again Kathleen" is about a man and his daughter trying to deal with the loss of a mother who died in the dentist chair. This happened to my friend Olive Swain's mother when we were about eleven. Terrifying to think your mother might go to the dentist and never come home.

Writing stories always felt good.

Then, at a writers' retreat at Fort Qu'Appelle, talk over lunch turned to imaginary friends. I hadn't had one unless you called the bear with the red eyes that lived under my bed and scared the bejeesus out of me every night, an imaginary enemy I guess.

Doris Larson, a Saskatoon artist, told the story about her friends' son, Oliver, who had an imaginary flock of chickens. He loved them but they caused him a lot of trouble, being numerous and hard to manage. And she told how his parents finally were able to help Oliver let go of them. It was brilliant.

It was a wonderful story. A gift of another children's story. Some time later I wrote the story in the back seat of David Carpenter's car going to Regina for our writers' group meeting. They were impressed but I'd had it all in my head for a while.

I talked to Oliver's parents and to Oliver himself, before sending the story to a publisher. The basic story was all true, and I had fun with the chickens, especially the head chicken, Doris, named for Doris

Larson. Doris – the chicken, that is – was a singer whose great-grandfather was a sea captain, and she enthusiastically sang sea shanties on the trip to the island, which would become a new home for the chickens.

Kim LaFave illustrated *Oliver's Chickens.* His illustrations were delightful, especially Doris peering in the teacher's ear at story time to see where the story was coming from. And all of the chickens hiding in the closet when Oliver's parents ordered Kentucky Fried Chicken.

Oliver, a teenager by then, came to the book launch in 1992. That was very special.

An interesting aside – Someone told my *Oliver's Chickens* story to Kim LaFave. I had submitted the story to Groundwood Books, an arm of Douglas & McIntyre, and they turned it down. Kim LaFave, a wonderful artist and Groundwood illustrator dug in his heels and said he was going to illustrate the book and we would take it to another publisher. They didn't want to lose their best illustrator and they took the book. They called it an Early Reader book, and published it in 1992. Thank you, Kim.

You Can't Miss It.
Wild Rose Country.

The two-week writing workshop at Cypress Hills Park in the fall of 1984 was over, the participants happy but ready after two weeks of nose-to-the-grindstone seclusion to pack up and head home. The park, on the highest point of land in Saskatchewan, was an unusual venue for a writers' workshop. Beautiful, with climate and vegetation similar to Banff National Park, but no pub nearby for everyone to scatter to in the evenings. Writers without a pub? It just didn't feel right, even for a non-drinker. No grocery store either. Civilization beckoned.

I had led a prose workshop. Elyse St. George, who had taken Patrick Lane's poetry workshop, was traveling with me. We had half a province to cover on the way to Saskatoon, so after an early lunch and good-byes we started off.

It was a special day for both of us. My book of short

stories, *Pictures*, would be launched that night by Fifth House, with the cover of Elyse's stunning painting "Hound Among the Poppies."

Elyse was working on a blue shawl and began to knit soon after we left Cypress Hills. It was a beautiful fall day, and we'd get home in plenty of time for dinner and a change of clothes. We were excited as we talked about the stories that always come out of a workshop with writers and novice writers, who was doing exciting work, who surprised most, who not so much. Funny incidents. And there were comfortable silences as Elyse knitted and I enjoyed the scenery.

One such silence was becoming quite long, while I began to wonder why none of the scenery looked familiar. That big, beautiful barn, I loved those barns. The farm with all the sheep, funny I didn't see that, animal lover that I was. Those beautiful horses. But then, I'd only passed them once when we were running late, caught off-guard by the sheer distance to the Cypress Hills. We had to be on the right road, didn't we?

Why I of all people should harbour that thought is beyond belief. On my many school visits I'd been lost more than I'd been not lost. But we were all right, the highway was good. But we'd been on it a long time. It was getting too dark for Elyse to knit, but everything was fine. It had to be fine. And on and on we went.

Do we have to go through Alberta to get to Saskatoon? Elyse said.

What?!

Do we have to go through Alberta to get to Saskatoon? That sign back there said Welcome to Wild Rose Country.

Oh. My. God. We were hopelessly lost. Forget the book launch. Caroline would kill me. If I was lucky. Elyse wisely didn't say anything as I U turned and we started back. I had no idea where we were or where we'd been. It was a long way back just to get to Cypress Hills Park and half a province from there. We'd be out of gas before long and maybe have to camp in the car. I hoped Elyse's shawl would cover us both.

Elyse was a geographically-challenged prairie passenger recently returned from New Hampshire, and I was a directionally-challenged driver. We might never see Saskatoon again.

Somewhere on that long dark drive back we saw a few lights and pulled into a tiny village with a gas pump. Just one very old gas pump in front of a small, square, peeling building. We were both desperate for a washroom.

Dim lights came from two or three house shapes through the trees. No electricity had reached there yet.

Let's try that house over there, Elyse said. A tall, narrow two-storey with a faint light somewhere inside. We stumbled over in the dark and knocked on the door. No answer. Knocked louder. No answer. Were those footsteps approaching? Someone shuffling closer? Psycho, Elyse whispered. The hair on my neck went up. We didn't know whether to laugh or scream. A fumbling and the door finally opened. An ancient man inspected us and didn't think much of what he saw. What? he said.

We need gas, I told him. Are you the service station man? A sigh and he reached down for his jacket and keys. Oh blessed relief. We mutually decided not to ask for use of his bathroom. We followed him back to the gas pump where he proceeded to push a long handle on the pump slowly back and forth, back and forth, like it was one of Hercules's labours, and gas bubbled up in the glass top. I had not seen a gas pump like that since very early Livelong days. This was feeling more and more like a time warp.

Could we use the washroom, please? Elyse asked.

He jerked a thumb over his shoulder. Back there.

'Back there' was an ancient toilet, dimly revealed by my cigarette lighter, long abandoned by humans and gleefully taken over by fat spiders, racing away from the dim light. The weeds behind the building looked downright inviting. Sanitary, even.

As we squatted there hoping there was no poison ivy which could be awkward should we ever get to the book launch, a kind of Oh, what the hell, what will be will be, took over and there in the weeds we laughed and laughed and laughed. It felt good.

Will we get to Saskatoon if we stay on this road? I asked the gas man. Oh, Saskatoon, he said, like he might say Oh, Montreal. Eventually, he said, hanging up the pump handle.

Well, we had a full tank of gas, we might make it all the way to Manitoba.

This was, of course, before the advent of cell phones, and we couldn't call Caroline and explain. I was glad since I'd once been on the receiving end of Caroline's temper and didn't want a rerun.

We paid for the gas and got back on the road. Our never-ending road to somewhere. The book launch started at eight o'clock. Forget that.

But we pulled into Saskatoon at eight and went straight to the launch in wrinkled workshop clothes, coffee-stained tee shirts, morning makeup long gone, blinking in the light like miners after hours and hours in the dark.

Caroline was delighted and relieved to see us, and there was a very nice turnout at the launch. They laughed at the story we had to tell. And there was food, which we sorely needed.

And best of all, our beautiful book, and posters of

the cover on the walls. I have never been as happy before or since about a book cover. Several people
bought the posters to frame.

Remembering this episode reminds me of a cartoon
I saw. A bearded, biblical-looking man met another
man on a path who looked like he'd been run over by
a herd of horses. Hey Job! called the first man. Con-
gratulations! I hear you got a book out.

Elyse and I still laugh about our time-travel experience. And now I wouldn't trade it for a sensible journey. I still laugh when I think of Elyse saying, Do we
have to go through Alberta to get to Saskatoon?

It seems we did.

Meeting Sergeant Wilson

One quiet day on my own at Westgate Books, I happened to notice on a circular metal rack the picture of a handsome Mounted Policeman on a short account called "Murder in Uniform." I picked it up and, back at my stool, read the story of the member of the early North-West Mounted Police (NWMP). Little did I know how this story would take over my life for several years.

It was the story of a Scot called John Wilson, who left his pregnant wife Polly and small son in Scotland and sailed to Canada in 1912 to try to find work and bring his family over.

This is not the way the story went. After different jobs he was hired by the North-West Mounted Police and stationed in the small town of Blaine Lake, not far from Saskatoon. There, six years after leaving home he fell madly in love with a young woman, Jessie Patterson. As I would learn later, that word "madly" is an understatement. He was besotted. He fell ill with

TB and was nursed by Jessie in the Patterson home. I envisioned a private upstairs bedroom, warm flowered wallpaper softly lit by a kerosene lamp. He was so ill he had expected to die, and when he didn't he proposed to Jessie.

Sergeant Wilson had conveniently decided he was not married. He was not the only man who divorced himself with an ocean, cheaper than a lawyer, and never looked back. However, this convenient out was not to be.

His letters home stopped, and fearing he was ill – his lungs were always weak – Polly boarded a ship and came to Canada. Her ship would have sailed through the north Atlantic at risk of German submarines during the last year of the war. A brave woman, or a foolhardy one.

I was rivetted by the story. Someone could have robbed the store and I wouldn't have noticed.

I had never heard about this event. There were, frustratingly, only the bare bones in that account, bare bones I would spend years putting meat on – a little fat here, a little more muscle there – but there was enough to leave me consumed with curiosity. It cried out for a book. It had everything, the iconic mounted police, a world war, a love triangle, the history of the time. What more could a writer ask?

Well, there was one more thing.

Murder.

This was a story that had to be told and with lots of fascinating background to enrich it. The Spanish flu, which killed millions of soldiers and civilians, would figure in it, as well as the early history of the RCMP, as the NWMP was renamed in 1920. I took the booklet and the only other copy home with me. I knew I had something very special and didn't want another writer stumbling on it.

I was working on a book of adult short stories at the time, and the Wilson story remained in my files for a couple of years. I had only a vague idea of how much research I faced, but knew I didn't even know where to begin.

Where to begin indeed. I wanted to make sure it would be published before I put in years of research so I called Rob Sanders, now at Greystone Books – his own imprint – in Vancouver and told him the story. He was intrigued and said, You write it and we will publish it. So far so good.

The Saskatchewan Archives in Regina seemed a logical place to begin. And that is where the first strange occurrence in a series of strange occurrences took place. I found almost nothing about the Sgt. Wilson story, just Polly's name on the passenger list of the *Mauretania*, the luxury ship on which her family had raised money for her passage because it was believed to be safe from German submarines. Her reason for going to Canada, given on the passenger list, was 'to join her mounted policeman husband.' Even that gave me a bit of a thrill, a feeling that someone – maybe Polly – was reaching out to me to tell her story.

I was ready to give up the second day in the Archives and was going to have lunch with Maggie Siggins when the girl who was trying to help me gave me a phone number. Someone else is interested in the story, she said, and I thought it was another writer working on the final chapter of my story. I think his interest is personal, she said. Why don't you give him a call.

I screwed up my courage and called a man who identified himself as Jessie Wilson's youngest son by her second marriage. He said he and his half-brother were trying to find out more about the story. When I told him my interest in the story, he said he wouldn't tell me anything. He was from a large family and if any of them knew he had even talked to me they would never speak to him again. I said I wanted to write the book because of the two women, and that his mother was a victim, also. He calmed down and said he would come over for coffee and we would talk about it. I told him I would even send him a copy of the book before it was published. I went for lunch.

When I told Maggie I'd told him he could read the book before it was published, Maggie screamed, No, no, no, you mustn't. If his family took exception to any part of the book they could get an injunction and hold up the publication for years. I was beginning to see that this was a whole different animal I had got hold of, and only the twitching tip of its tail. I was as ignorant as they come about nonfiction. And a totally inexperienced researcher to boot.

Jessie's son, a high school teacher in Regina, met me for coffee, and he told me more than he perhaps intended to. He said he'd been in high school when his girlfriend said something about him having a half brother. When he said he didn't have a half brother she told him other people in town said so. The town was Biggar. And the half brother, the oldest in the family, was John Wilson's son, Lindsay, who was born on the day his father was hanged for Polly's murder.

Now if you wrote that in fiction no one would believe it.

The teacher's mother, Jessie, had six more children and was involved in some community activities, he told me – she wrote for the local paper sometimes and helped in the church. But he also told me that his mother would withdraw from the family once a year, spending a day or more in her room. They never knew why, their father just carrying on without her. Perhaps they were on anniversaries of the day Wilson was hanged. I was later told by an old woman in Biggar that Jessie was shunned by many in the town and that some people crossed the street if they saw her coming. It was cruel. She hadn't murdered anybody.

I spoke to Glenn Wright, the historian at the RCMP headquarters in Ottawa and he gave me the numbers of the Wilson files in the Capital Crimes section of the National Archives. Murder is a capital crime. The Writers Union of Canada, to which I belonged at the time, was having its AGM in Ottawa and would pay members' way to attend. I jumped on that. Upon arrival in Ottawa I called to see if they had those files in the main archives there and luckily they did – they could have been kept in another city as the Archives in Ottawa was running out of room.

I got to only one Writers Union meeting. Spending three days at the Archives was an incredible experience. I was at times horrified, at times in tears, at the pleading letters from Polly's sister in Scotland to NWMP Superintendent Horrigan – and later Assistant Commissioner W.H Routledge – begging for news of Polly. Her letters had stopped and no one knew where she was or what had happened to her. The policemen's replies were unfailingly kind and hopeful until it was clear something was indeed wrong.

In reading through those documents I was more and more impressed with the quality of the men on that force. Many of them from England and Scotland. Their handwriting and hand-drawn maps were elegant. I also came to admire and like Polly's family, especially her brother, Jim, who called a spade a spade and John Wilson a scoundrel; and Polly herself, a good, generous soul. I flagged over 200 pages requesting copies be sent to me. I regret that I didn't include the police's coded telegrams from when they were trying to keep Wilson from running. It would have been fun for readers to try to break the code.

Two weeks later the documents arrived. I was committed. And scared. In the meantime I had made a trip to Blaine Lake and was unable to find anyone who could tell me where Polly was buried. Or indeed anyone inclined to talk about the case.

I wrote the sample chapters Rob Sanders had requested, using information from the files and dramatizing some scenes where, for example, police interviewed town people and using dialogue that would be probable in those situations. I gave no characters thoughts or dialogue unsupported by evidence. In other words I wrote it in the style I felt brought that time to life. I thought it was good. And waited to hear.

And waited.

Weeks.

Finally Rob called and said that I must write a strictly nonfiction account, and could not create scenes or dialogue.

I was enormously disappointed but could not dissuade him. So I set about writing a straight nonfiction account of the whole story. But I was bored and unable to resist dramatizing scenes of the murder, Wilson's marriage to Jessie, and one or two others.

A year later I sent it away and waited. Even longer this time. When Rob finally called, it was to say it was boring and the parts they really liked were the wedding and the murder and the other parts I had dramatized. I cried and couldn't stop crying. He was asking for the book I had started to write in the first place. It was a very long, very wet phone call. And I was back to square one. A wasted year. After I gave up trying to find a hit man to off Rob Sanders I got to work again. I still loved Rob, but wanted to kill him.

I don't want to know how much later I finally finished

the book, how many years it had taken, much of it filled with difficult-to-track-down research. Some of it so interesting I wanted to write about it at length: the Great War, the TB epidemic, the Spanish flu. The early days of the NWMP/RCMP and the Saskatchewan Provincial Police, a police force brought together by a fascinating man, Superintendent Charles Augustus Mahony, to relieve the enormity of the task facing the Northwest Mounted Police during the war when many of their rank had gone overseas.

While I was working on the book I temporarily rented my basement suite to a friend, a writer going through a divorce, and on his occasional visits for tea, he found me almost buried in the detritus of writing, revising, researching, going half blind trying to read reports of the trial on library microfiche which had faded to illegibility on the edges. For that I needed a magnifying glass and there were days when I wondered if I would ever write The End. Bill and I were both under a lot of stress, and neither of us ever left the house without coming back at least once for some forgotten thing. Doors slamming in unison sometimes.

Close to the end of the book, I went to Regina to work on the last bit, and to do some revisions at my friend Byrna Barclay's. My Toronto editor and I were disagreeing about some things and I was going a bit mad. It was past time to be finished.

Driving down I burned out the motor of my car, not realizing the fan belt had broken. Smoke poured out from under the hood and a kind trucker called the towing business in Davidson. Big Nick gave me what-for all the way back to Davidson. Didn't you see any red lights? he demanded. Not unless you count flames, I said.

He owned the garage there, with an adjoining coffee

shop. I sat dismally in the coffee shop waiting the results of his examination and wishing I had a cigarette. I had quit smoking, not good timing. When he motioned me from the doorway I knew I was in trouble. You have killed your car, he said, and I reached over and took the cigarette package out of his shirt pocket. He knew a woman on the edge when he saw one. He lit the cigarette for me.

When I finally reached Regina, in the back seat of a car with two fighting kids, Byrna explained the problem succinctly: put the research into the story, not the story into the research. Of course, I was so in love with some of the stuff I'd learned about the Spanish flu, and the TB epidemic and the war I was in danger of losing sight of the story. It takes another pair of eyes sometimes, and Byrna is a writer and a good editor.

One small aside – the complete file went missing from Byrna's computer when she was out one evening. I paced and cried and smoked, and smoked and cried and paced till she got home. She sat up half the night till she found the missing file. That's a friend.

By the time I went home the book was finished. It was spring and the book would be out in the fall. But apparently I would not be writing The End quite yet.

Trip to Scotland

My son Scott, now a journalist working in Russia for the CBC, came home for a quick visit. With him he brought a return ticket to Scotland. Mom, you have to go and see the places you're writing about. And of course he was right. What was the view from that little village Polly left to come to Canada to find her husband? Could you see Tinto Hill from there? What did it look like? What was the village like? Is my description of her carrying her sewing three miles down the long hill from Kilkeggie to Carluke accurate? What were the predominant flowers and shrubs? I should see the drapery shop in Carluke where Polly had fallen in love with Jack. Was it still there?

And so I set off.

I went soon after to be there in time for changes to the manuscript. I was excited, I'd never been to Europe. It was very early spring and my friends said, Pack warm, the damp cold goes right to your bones. So I did. And roasted in very warm weather. Having to do a lot of walking was torture until I broke down and bought a thin cotton blouse I could rinse out at night.

The plane landed in Glasgow, and I took the bus to Edinburgh, closer to the places I needed to see. I was struck by the lack of trees on that bus ride; I'd expected something different. The bus driver gave me a short history lesson on the way. That is where the early Christians met in secret, he told me, waving his arm off to the left somewhere. They risked jail, and sometimes their lives. And I thought about the cool way early Christians identified others, how in speaking to someone they weren't sure about, they would casually mark with a foot a curve in the sand, and if the other person completed the symbol with a reverse curve, a symbol of the fish, they were also Christian. Shorthand for the story of Jesus feeding the multitudes. The Scots were probably short of sand but they managed somehow.

I stayed in a small hotel in the Grassmarket area of Edinburgh, The Thistle Inn. It had originally been a home, or temporary home, for people on the street. It was great – friendly staff, a small, shiny-clean room with a sink and small shower, nice window. And a bar downstairs where a wonderful Irish band played most nights.

Across from the Inn was a small raised dark flat rock where apparently people were hanged back in the day. A plaque told the story of a woman who was hanged twice and lived to tell the tale. Ever after she was known as "Twice Hung Whatever her name was."

The area still had a lot of homeless people who seemed to be having the time of their lives. Maybe because it was spring. My hotel room looked across at a building with a large room that was lit every night, where people could drop in, get a cup of coffee and relax for a while. People came and went there, most of them seemed to know each other, or so it seemed by the greetings. Then off they'd go, waving as they passed the window and disappearing into the night, looking like people with plans. There was one particular pair, an old bearded man and a young frizzy-red-haired woman, always together, and always looking pleased as Punch about something.

I wanted to know if anyone from the Sergeant Wilson story was still alive. For two days I walked from the Inn down to a long, grassy area with the Castle on the hill up to the right – Ian Rankin territory – to the Endinburgh New Register House. And found in their archives when the main characters – I felt I knew them – had died, and discovered that John Wilson's daughter, who was born after he left Scotland, was still alive. That was exciting. I found her address and phone number in Carluke and wondered if it might be possible to meet her, but how to approach her? She was an old woman now.

Scott kept track of me with nightly phone calls from Russia and I told him my dilemma, how could I just arrive at this old woman's doorstep and ask about something so sensitive. Here's what you do, he said, write her a letter saying you are there researching events in Saskatchewan in 1918, and if she would like to call you this is your number. Leave the letter at her house and then it's her choice whether to call or not.

I spent another day researching, trying to find newspaper reports about Polly's murder and the trial. Staff at the New Register House directed me to The Edinburgh Central Library, inside like something out of Dickens, or earlier, but with no luck. After doing a few tourist things, not wanting to leave the Thistle Inn, I took a bus to Carluke.

Carluke was where Polly worked as a seamstress

and fell in love with John Wilson, a tailor at the store. Apparently it had been love at first sight for John Wilson, that passionate fellow. He alarmed Polly's family when he declared that if he wasn't allowed to marry Polly he would kill himself. The good, sensible Hutchison family had reservations, particularly her older brother, Jim, who would later say, when Polly seemed to go missing in Canada, that he never trusted John Wilson any farther than he could throw him. Wilson had, in fact, left Scotland under a cloud, having stolen money to help his brother Alex, who ran the family business. It failed anyway.

The tailor store was still there on the corner and I looked in the window. It probably didn't look much different than when they worked there. Unfortunately it was Easter and everything was closed. I should have anticipated that when I booked the flight. An experienced researcher would have.

However I saw the long hill Polly walked down from Kilkeggie to the tailor shop, with sewing she did for the manager, supporting herself and her children when money and letters from Wilson stopped. The manager gave her all the work he could. He felt sorry for Polly but he also said she was the best seamstress he ever had. She was, at that time, sewing a lot of widows' dresses, as so many local men were dying in the war. The black wreath on the tailor's door just one of many.

My landlady at the bed and breakfast drove me up to the village where John and Polly had lived, and from where they had both left, separately, to come to Canada. It was a wildly windy day, not unusual, the woman said. The village was actually named Kilnkadzow, called Kilkeggie by everyone.

It was all there. The old stone houses with their low stone walls, like a place frozen in time. A film company easily could have gone in there and told Polly's

272

and John's story at little cost. I knocked on a couple of those doors, expecting and hoping to find some old person who knew the story. No answer at one, two doors were opened by yuppies, who wanted to fix up a piece of the past, and who tried to be helpful but who had never heard the story. On the far side of the village old people had left the stone houses for modern bungalows, and central heating. No help there either. People who lived there now didn't give a hoot about history but loved the views and the quiet life.

On the walk back down to Carluke, I imagined Polly, struggling in that wind, trying to keep her finished work from blowing away. I passed strawberry fields and homes with people growing strawberries in their yards for the jam factory. And the jam factory. And the windmill where John and Polly liked to walk. I loved the Scots, who were always up for a gab about what they were doing, or what you were doing. And they called everyone luv, which I liked. My mother's family came from Scotland, and I felt proud to be a Scot.

And off in the distance was the majestic Tinto Hill, mauve and wine and purple with heather, beautiful in light and shadow. Scott was right, it was important to see and feel it all.

In Carluke I saw the stone church where John and Polly were married. The school she'd attended. The graves of her brother, Jim, her sister Elizabeth, her brother in law, Archie. All people who had loved Polly. Her son, George, just three when she left, was also there. Where Polly should have been.

The phone call came. Polly's daughter called me. And she was angry. Why are you writing about that awful thing? I said I was sorry she felt that way. I wanted to write her mother's story. Why would you want to write about her? Evidently Polly had not been forgiven for leaving her and her brother. I wanted her to be remembered, I said, because she was a good person and a terrible thing happened to her. That she'd been so brave.

Oh, brave, is that what you call it? Have you any idea what it was like for me and my brother growing up with that story? I think it must have been very hard, and I'm sorry, I said. It was always there, she said. The talk. And then she didn't sound quite so angry.

I was able to ask her a few questions. Had she lived all her life in Carluke? Yes, she had. What had George done? George had been a schoolteacher and died quite young. Neither married. I wanted to ask if he remembered his father but I didn't – he was three when his father left and they were always together, John apparently a very good father. But also very good at forgetting he had a son when it suited him. Then her anger came back. I will never read that book. I don't want anyone here to read it. No, I said, that was unlikely, it would just be published in Canada. I thanked her for talking to me, and shortly after, she hung up.

I got lost at least once a day, so got to talk to a lot of people. A lot of friendly, red-haired people. Once I didn't listen to directions well enough, a bad habit, and ended up near dark down in a large warehouse area. The sidewalk was incredibly narrow, two people could not walk abreast, and the traffic shot past terrifyingly fast on the very wide street.

I didn't have a clue where I was, or where Grassmarket and the Thistle Inn were. In some of the alleys people were dealing drugs, or it certainly looked like that's what they were doing, and they looked like they were having fun. I was starting to get worried when I spied a man in a light trench coat walking ahead. I caught up to him and asked if I could walk close behind him, I was lost. Eyeing his trench coat belt wanting to hang onto it.

Oh, Grassmarket, that's where I'm going, too, just follow me. Where are we? I asked and he told me it was the road the horses from the palace had used. I could imagine them galloping madly past, sometimes two and four abreast, carriages rocking in their wake. He took me all the way to Grassmarket, in sight of the Inn, then turned around with a little wave and smile and went back the way we'd come.

Every day I bought the Edinburgh newspaper. There was a nice nook at the end of the upstairs hall with a comfortable chair, lamp and side table, and a different view out the window. I looked forward to sitting down there and reading the paper. I hadn't walked so much in a long time. There was a story one night that I still remember. A young woman was applying for social assistance. The worker asked, Do you think it was wise to put F All in this space for income? Well, there wasn't room to write family allowance, the girl replied.

One of the highlights was a trip to the Edinburgh Zoo to see the Penguin Walk, daily at 2 p.m. On the bus to the zoo we passed an old flatiron building on a corner and two women said, There's the old Binns Store. These were my relatives on my dad's side, my grandfather Binns's brothers, who had a large, beautiful Binns Department Store in downtown Edinburgh that I didn't know about and missed seeing. Unfortunately there wasn't time, I was leaving the next day. But I saw it online and it was impressive.

I found the penguin enclosure at the zoo; it seemed to go on forever, with ponds and rocky areas, and penguins, penguins everywhere. There were the commonly known black and white penguins, some with warm yellow and orange trim, and some with comical spiky orange feathers on their heads, who seemed to be constantly shaking their heads madly, as if trying to get rid of them. Others swam as if competing in Penguin Olympics. I especially liked watching the expectant fathers shuffling along with large eggs on their feet, checking often to see their eggs were safe. After walking around for a while, I headed back to the penguins, in lots of time for the famous penguin walk.

I started watching one old fellow who was having a hard time staying awake. His head would drop forward a bit and he'd shake himself and straighten up, over and over again; it became clear that he was trying to stay awake for something. And then one, then two, then more, including him, started to waddle from every part of the huge enclosure in the direction of a wide gate. By 2 o'clock – the time of the walk – there were about fifty of them lined up at the gate.

On the dot of two a young guy hopped up and opened the tall gate and the penguins shuffled out. Then in rows of three or four they waddled and wambled (good Scottish word) along the path that ran around the zoo, a lot of us walking along beside the path. I can't explain it, but there was something so *sweet, so dear* about those penguins going for a walk. I had also gone to see The Castle, but the Penguin Walk beat the castle, hands – or webbed-feet – down.

My first and only trip overseas was very interesting. I came home with vivid pictures in my mind and a feel for the places and people. And there was time to do some revisions, which made the book better. The Scottish people made me happy to be one of them.

The Secret Lives of Sgt. John Wilson

Prologue

Saskatchewan, 1918

In a dark office building on Scarth Street in Regina, a ninth floor window is lit, as it often is these cold December nights. Superintendent Charles Augustus Mahony is working late. The second annual report of the Saskatchewan Provincial Police to the attorney general is due, and there is much to report: more than a thousand assaults, five hundred thefts, eight murders, the lists go on and on. Gusts of icy wind buffet the building. Through a curtain of drifting snow, the light in the window burns on.

In a shallow grave in a culvert near Waldheim, thirty miles from Saskatoon, lies the body of a young woman, almost six months pregnant. She is dressed in a blue tweed suit of fine-quality British wool, beautifully handmade, and a navy coat. On the shoulder of the suit, stained dark with blood, is the remnant of a corsage. She is wrapped in a coarse wool car robe.

As Charles Mahony works late in his Regina office, the December snows drift higher over the grave, which is somewhat protected from the sweep of freezing winds by the culvert. Now and then on the road above, a team of horses pulls muffled figures through the night on their way to or from Waldheim; an occasional Model T rattles and coughs its way to the city, perhaps for a medical emergency, perhaps piloted by a bachelor desperate for the sight of a human face, any place other than an isolated prairie shack with frost riming the cracks in the walls. Apart from these passing disturbances, there are only the sounds of wind and drifting snow, the snapping of twigs in the frigid air, and, in the long, star-hung nights, a coyote's yelp, the soft hoot of an owl.

The couple renting rooms at 217 9th Street in Saskatoon seem very much in love. They moved into the handsome rooming house on October 1, and were often seen walking in the mellow fall evenings, or driving in a new Grey Dort. He wears the uniform of the Military Police, which suits his slim frame and craggy good looks. But to an astute observer, the marks of a recent illness are discernible; a certain pale fragility and the drawn, listening expression of one attuned to slight shifts from within. His young wife's solicitous manner supports this observation. They have eyes only for each other, though at times her loving glances find him deep in sombre thought.

Perhaps he is not well. There is reason for concern; the flu that ravaged Europe has arrived, the first cases reported in the east. Or perhaps he is just homesick for Scotland.

The woman in the shallow grave knows no more loving glances. She will never see her home again.

Charles Mahony is pleased with the fledgling police force he had so hastily assembled to begin law enforcement in January, 1917. The Attorney General's order to form a provincial force in just twenty five days launched a mission that at the outset seemed nearly impossible. But Mahony raided police forces across the country, and he had an eye for good prospects, he once saw two men laying bricks in Regina and hired them on the spot.

And now Mahoney has reason to feel proud of the record emerging from his Underwood typewriter; a

chronicle of hundreds of minor offenses and griev-
ances discreetly but thoroughly handled, and myriad
patrols from ten to one hundred miles and more.
Sometimes hundreds of miles are covered to investi-
gate a death, only to find that the person died of natural causes.

The woman under the culvert did not die of natural
causes. No one is investigating her death.

Mahony leans back and runs a hand over his bald
head, his keen dark eyes looking beyond the green
painted wall cluttered with memos. The original rag-
gle-taggle band, formed to relieve the enormity of the
task facing the Royal North-West Mounted Police,
has grown to 106 men, sixty-two of whom are ex-
Mounties and another twenty-four have experience in
police forces throughout the world. A professional,
proud force gaining the respect of the people.

They call him Manny at his suggestion because he
hates being called Mahoney, (no one pronounces it
right – Ma-ha-ny) and he knows that behind his back
the men affectionately call him Charles Augustus. The
good reputation of this force is no small accomplish-
ment, considering the population of the province is
782,267, which averages out at one law enforcer for
every 7,379 people. To say nothing of the logistics of
covering so large a territory – 250,000 square miles.

And the population is still growing, a steady stream
arriving from everywhere it seems; men with land in
their eyes, entrepreneurial schemes in their heads.
Some will succeed, some fail. And some will turn to
crime. Nothing they do will surprise Charles Mahony
much. In thirty years of police work, he has seen it all.

In the silent building the typewriter clatters on: cattle thefts; indecent assaults; arson; robbery; child neglect; murder.

One murder is not recorded.

The pile of papers on the oak desk is sizable, he is almost finished. Mahony gets up to stretch and look out the window. Smoke from the chimneys hangs momentarily in the frigid air, then dissipates with a gust of wind. A muffled figure leaning into the wind passes under a street light. A hard place, this Saskatchewan, and big enough to be a country. But interesting. Always that.

He returns to his chair, picks up the pile of papers and taps it on the desk to straighten it. A record of good men fulfilling their duties with courage and growing maturity. Other good men will be coming home from the war. He looks forward to finding some excellent recruits among their numbers. Whatever 1919 holds, it will not be dull. Of that he can be sure.

The job is done until next year. The light in the upstairs window goes out, and Charles Mahony heads home for a few hours sleep.

The Stories I Missed

The *Saskatoon Star Phoenix* review began with this: *The book has everything, a love triangle, a handsome rogue, the TB and Spanish flu epidemics, and the settling of the west, all played out against the background of a world war.*

They published an excerpt from the book: I chose the car trip and the stop at a culvert under the guise of shooting geese, and the scene leading up to the moment that was poor Polly Wilson's last.

Supply ran out well before Christmas. People like true crime stories. Good reviews arrived. The book was good. All that effort rewarded.

Almost the day after the *Star Phoenix* review, I got a call from an old gentleman called Henry Neufeld, who said, My dad and I were the first people to see that policeman that day. He came weaving up to the farm wanting a drink of water and told us his car was on fire down at the culvert. I'll never forget it. I'd never seen a policeman and I had never seen a burning car before. Never seen a car before. He was white as a sheet and puked in my mother's lilac bush. It was exciting to talk to someone who was a part of the story.

After Polly's murder the place was crawling with policemen – NWMP, the SPP (Saskatchewan Provincial Police) and the Saskatoon City Police – none of whom were able to find Polly's grave under the culvert. That was hard to understand. And a call had been put out to the citizenry to keep an eye out for a fresh grave, and people with shovels were scouring the countryside. There was a kind of exhilarating, holiday atmosphere to the search.

A week or two after the book came out I got a call about this search. Another old man said, My mother knew all along where that body was buried. Every time she tried to take her horse to town after that it would rear at the culvert and refuse to go a step further. Even a whipping would not make it budge. What an amazing picture. Later I wrote a screenplay about the Sgt. Wilson story and used that as the opening scene.

I had many more calls about the book, but those two stick in my mind.

I was asked to read and discuss the book with grade twelve students, a nice change from the little people who always asked how old I was and how many cats did I have. The book was subsequently included in the grade twelve curriculum as a supplementary reading choice. I credit the grade twelve teacher Mark Wildeman for that. I still receive a nice royalty cheque twice a year. I'm very glad I saw John Wilson on that book rack.

One last thing.

I got a phone call from Rob Sanders to tell me the book had been nominated as the nonfiction choice by the Crime Writers of Canada. It was great to have the book in the running for a national prize. And then the *Macleans* review came out and Scott called and said, Mom, don't read that review. It will make you feel bad.

Of course I read it and it made me feel bad.

It was reviewed with a nonfiction book by a Toronto writer – also nominated for the prize – about a local policeman who had thrown his wife to her death from a balcony. The reviewer made no bones about which would win, and was unbearably patronizing about my book and about what I had previously written – a bunch of kids' books and something called *Betty Lee Bonner Lives There*. It was the most negative, supercilious review I've ever read. Anywhere.

I was staying with a friend in Langley, B.C. when the awards gala took place in Vancouver but decided not to go, in no small part because of that review. I didn't want to see that reviewer or the other writer celebrating. Oh me of little faith.

Winning the Crime Writers of Canada Arthur Ellis Award for Nonfiction was very sweet.

Meeting Got To Go

It was late in the summer and I was editing *The Doll*, the second children's book by Cora Taylor, a children's writer from Alberta. I had also edited her first book, *Julie*. I knew that book was special when I first read it and happily accepted the job as editor for her next. *Julie* had won the Governor General's Award for children's literature.

Now *The Doll* needed more work before publishing and we were late. This makes a publisher nervous. And a bit testy. Cora and I were delivered to the Sylvia Hotel in Vancouver and told not to come out until the book was finished.

Staying in the Sylvia Hotel for the first time is a great experience. The hotel walls are completely covered in thickly woven Virginia creeper, and you're given a bag of peanuts to feed the squirrels that run around the ivy. Sometimes racoons climb up, the ivy is so dense and strong, and might peek hopefully in your window.

Through that window the outdoors beckon. English Bay sparkles in the sun, the beach right across the street. Popcorn leaping in the red popcorn cart there. The seawall path that leads to Stanley Park.

All pleasures for another time. Work called.

Cora and I fell in love with the Sylvia Hotel. Who could not? The location, its cozy lobby, the great staff, and a resident cat. We were both animal lovers, and the Sylvia allowed dogs. I had visited Cora on her farm outside Edmonton, where she kept lots of four-footed friends including a pet donkey, and we had become friends.

We did leave the Sylvia as much as we dared, and often in coming or going saw the large grey cat who seemed to own the place. He slept on the red striped chairs in the lobby and sometimes a guest would look longingly at the chair and then settle for one less comfortable. He also slept on the wide windowsill in the lobby – the cat, not the guest – watching the goings-on outside. He liked to watch the dogs chasing sticks into the water, over and over and over. Probably thought they were stupid.

I adore cats and have always had a furry roommate – elegant pure black Kato who fell in love with a little visiting tabby and acted very silly when she was around; big orange Molly, who liked to walk down the middle of the street and it was the cars that had to stop; and my adored tortoise shell Alice, a bossy, noisy broad who suited me to a T. She was my last cat, and I will always miss her.

The Sylvia Hotel cat was almost an exact replica of Tommy, my very first cat, a small, bedraggled stray who came to my dad's elevator when I was in grade one and was still alive when my daughter Anne was born. He was Old Tom by then.

One day when Cora and I came back from lunch, Old Tom's lookalike was batting around some wool belonging to the desk clerk.

What's his name, I asked. Got To Go, she said. That's his *name*? Yes. How long has he been here? Seven years. She rolled her eyes.

From this meeting Cora went to her room to work. On *The Doll*, I devoutly hoped, as I wrote the first Got To Go story, worrying that Cora might be doing the same thing. I was excited and somehow knew it was special. It's that falling in love again all over. It's there in all good work. The next morning at breakfast I read the Got To Go story to Cora and received an enthusiastic response.

Soon after, with regret, we finished our job and went our separate ways. *The Doll* also won an award.

After revision – though it needed very little, a word here and there, it seemed to come of a piece – I submitted Got To Go to Red Deer Press. Editor Tim Wynne-Jones responded quite soon with a warm acceptance and Got To Go was on his way. Apparently there was another children's book called *Got To Go* so we added the *Mister*. And it feels right now.

I knew that a Vancouver artist, Cynthia Nugent, was illustrating *Mister Got To Go*. I had never seen her work and hoped to get a glimpse of the process. My glimpse was a very dark Xerox that didn't tell me much. Then the book arrived with wonderful, vibrant illustrations so far beyond my imaginings.

There was no doubt where this book was set. It was the Sylvia Hotel right down to the tiniest detail. And Got To Go was perfect, every expression just right – how is that possible, I wonder? – even his back when he looked out the window at the foolish dogs chasing sticks in the rain told you how he is feeling. He was perfect. She was a cat person, no doubt about that.

Hell, no, she said, when I called her. I had to rent one from the SPCA, and it was so vicious I was afraid to go home. The only time I could draw it was when it was asleep. I think we became friends with that first phone call.

The other characters in the book, Mister Foster, the manager, Miss Pritchett, the desk clerk, the cook, Old Harry the bellhop, even the hotel guests, come alive. The illustrations took *Mister Got To Go* over the top. Good illustrators do that. Cynthia is a brilliant illustrator.

We did two more Got To Go books together. They won awards, and were starred choices by the Canadian Children's Book Centre. Cynthia was chosen second in a competition for Canadian illustrators.

It's not really fair that writer and illustrator share the royalties equally. Something I wrote in an afternoon would take Cynthia many months to illustrate. For a ten-dollar soft-cover, we each get fifty cents. Or sometimes forty cents. We don't do it to get rich, but it's still unfair, though I doubt that will ever change.

If the response to *Mister Got To Go* was amazing, so was the response of the Sylvia Hotel to the book. Beyond amazing. They took it to heart. When teachers gave notice classrooms of children were coming to see the Sylvia and hoping to catch a glimpse of Got To Go, the kitchen had gallons of hot chocolate ready. And each child went home with a paper doily signed *Mister Foster* – the name of the manager in the books – by the real manager, Axel DeVeriere, and stamped with a cat paw print.

Kids' illustrations of the story arrived regularly at the Sylvia, and a *Kids' Got To Go* gallery bloomed in the back entrance to the hotel.

You Can't Miss It. Paynton.

It was a long trip to do readings at Paynton School and Lloydminster, I'd hardly slept the night before, and really, really didn't want to go. But there was no way out.

I'd never been to Paynton so was grateful for the first familiar 120-mile trip to North Battleford. It will always be miles to me, and pounds, too, I haven't made a meat loaf since they changed to metric. I'm like the woman who went into a fabric store and asked if a kilometer of this material would be enough to make a dress. To which the clerk replied, It depends on whether or not you want long sleeves.

Anyway, judging by the map – for once I had one – from North Battleford to Paynton was farther than Saskatoon to North Battleford, and then a trip from Paynton to Lloydminster. And home again. God knows how many miles in all. The Lloydminster reading was for adults, in something called the Plan-etarium. Maybe I'd be peering at them through a for-est. Sitting on a tree branch.

And where the devil was Paynton? I'd been driving forever and would have to cross the river on a ferry. I remember Dad talking about the Paynton Ferry, even had a faint recollection of going across it with him, but maybe not, since where would we have been going?

And then, oh lovely lovely sign, "PAYNTON FERRY." And there it was, the river not very wide at that point, so it shouldn't take long. I was almost run-ning late. A large man stood on the ferry with his hand on a large lever. A man you could trust to get you where you're going. I drove down and onto the ferry, and smiled at the big ferry man. The day was getting better.

He threw the lever and we began to move. This was going to be fun.

Where to? he yelled over the ferry noise. An odd question surely, since we were only going across the river.

Paynton, I called, over the din of the ferry.

What? He jammed the big lever the other way, holding it hard. *Paynton?* he said, like he'd never heard of the place. You don't get to *Paynton* this way. We slowly juddered to a stop and started going back.

Well, where is Paynton?

Down the road. The way you were going. Rolling his eyes. I didn't like that. He didn't look any smarter than I did.

Back to the landing, where fortunately no cars were waiting to prevent my backing out and turning around on the not very wide approach.

I waved. He didn't wave back.

Finally, not Paynton, but Paynton School appeared

on the left, on a kind of rise. It was strange, sitting there all by itself like a mirage, but I was frazzled and maybe somehow missed seeing the town. I'll never know now.

Had I ever been this tired? But teachers always feed you and that made me feel a little better. Then we discussed the reading. The teachers said how excited the kids were.

Grades three and four, right?

Oh, no. Kindergarten to grade eight, they said. I wanted to cry.

No. How can I do all those ages? I'll do grades two to five. Or six, I said, seeing frowns. That I might survive, grade six would enjoy some of the black humour poems.

They laughed merrily. Oh, you'll do just fine. We've heard how good you are. We can't disappoint them now. Why the hell not, I wanted to say, but it would be no use. The teachers wanted a little holiday from teaching and they were going to have it.

I don't think I can do it. Kids from four to fifteen. Taking a year off kindergarten and adding an extra year on the grade eights.

They laughed some more, but with side glances at each other. *The ingrate. After we were nice enough to ask her to come. She sounded all right on the phone. Yes, and she's being paid, you know. Quite a lot. And now she doesn't want to do it. She doesn't look very good, maybe got a mental problem.*

I survived. Kindergarten kids screeched and ran around, and the grade eights talked and laughed the whole time, a couple of the teachers, too.

It was the only school I left not loving the teachers.

Now. On to Lloydminster and the Planetarium. Maybe I'd be reading on Mars. It was going to be all right wherever; I liked talking to adults about the

Sergeant Wilson story, almost all women at afternoon readings. The women always got mad at John Wilson. And after another long drive, or maybe it only seemed long, I was in Lloydminster, looking for someone on the street to ask.

I drove around till I saw people leaving a Seniors Hall and heading – very slowly – to cars in the parking lot beside the Hall. I stopped at the top of a very gentle slope and caught up with an old couple in the parking lot.

Excuse me, could you direct me to the Planetarium? I asked the woman.

The what?

The Planetarium?

The what? Like I'd asked the way to the moon. Maybe I was – moon, planetarium.

What's she want? the old man asked.

I don't know, she said, I can't understand her.

The PLANETARIUM, upping the volume and standing closer. The LIBRARY, I shouted.

What'd she say?

I don't know. I can't understand her. Something about berries.

About *what*?

I don't *know*. I can't under...

I wanted to kill them but there wasn't time. My car was going down the hill without me.

I ran. Stop! Stop!

It had slowed down when I yanked open the door and fell in. A woman on the next street directed me to the library.

The librarian knew a desperate woman when she saw one, taking me into a nice room where I collapsed in a comfortable chair.

I'm sorry I'm late.

It's all right.

Tears came. I'm sorry, I'm having a bad day.

That's all right. She took me to the washroom. Just take your time. I'll go tell them you're here and need a few minutes. Would you like some coffee?

Sometimes blush and lipstick and a comb can do wonders. And sometimes not. Coffee was the magic elixir. And a refill for the reading. Some energy trickling into my veins.

The audience was great. Lots of questions about Sergeant Wilson, the rat. They hated him. I knew they would.

The librarian gave me muffins and coffee for the road, and a nice warm hug.

A stop for gas and I was on the way home. Some days are just better than other days.

p.s. Okay, it's time for the funniest joke I have ever heard.

A minister out for a walk was asked by a woman if he would speak to the church's women's group. He said he thought he could, what would they like him to talk about. The woman said they'd like him to talk about sex.

At dinner before his talk, his wife asked him what he was going to talk to the ladies about. He said he was going to talk about sailing.

The next day at a grocery lineup one of the ladies said to his wife, Your husband gave the most wonderful talk last night.

Oh, his wife said, I don't know why he wanted to talk about that. He's only done it twice and the first time he threw up and the second time his cap blew off.

Unknowables. Ghosts.

It was another writers' retreat, this time back at Fort San, the site of the Saskatchewan Summer School of the Arts. We were lodged in one of the old TB hospital buildings, which had housed so many poor souls infected in the TB epidemic of the 30s and 40s. The disease was highly communicable and, before antibiotics, there was no known cure. Treatment mostly consisted of being wheeled out into the large verandahs for most of the day – sometimes on see-your-breath days. It was believed that fresh air, food, rest, and sometimes removal of certain ribs to facilitate lung expansion, had the best outcomes. The stories are many.

The undertaker, Mister Stiff, (no kidding) was in the morgue directly below the children's ward. How could they have done that? A tall fence around the "children's bin" helped prevent escapes. Every time a patient died, the bell on a tall tower rang. It rang often and patients would guess who was gone. They developed a black humour about the place – if ribs were served with dinner, they joked about whose they were.

I was told some of these things by a woman who wrote a book about her experiences there, *Valley of the Flowers*, a very well-written account. Her name was Veronica Brock.

Veronica was diagnosed with TB at age sixteen in the TB trailer, which travelled all over the province. She writes about her fear traveling by bus to Fort Qu'Appelle; she'd never been away from home. Her fear of being separated from her family. Her fear of dying.

After spending several years at the sanitarium and having two or more ribs removed, it was discovered that she had not had TB when she arrived. She had it before she left. A ghastly mistake.

What was most powerful in the book was how she kept her spirits up year after year, bedridden and lonely for her family. She apparently made the best of it, her bright personality and sense of humour obviously a gift to herself and other patients. I was especially struck by her lack of self-pity about those years. I assume I would be a sniveling wreck but maybe we can't know until we're tested.

When Veronica was finally discharged in her early twenties, she was told she must never have children, not strong enough for childbirth or to raise children. She promptly put paid to that. She married and had six children. And became a writer.

At this hospital-ward retreat were Patrick Lane and Lorna Crozier, Byrna Barclay, David Carpenter, Edna Alfred, Gertrude Story, Kate Bitney - Anne Szumigalski's daughter from Winnipeg – and Reg Silvester. Most of them I knew well from the Summer School classes at the same facility. There were one or two other writers there too, I think.

We settled in, choosing our rooms – you tried to get there early to get your favourite – and setting up our work spaces, unpacking books and whatever else needed for two weeks of hard work.

We gathered in the lounge the first night, caught up on news, talked about what we were working on, had a few drinks. Ginger ale for me, always bloody ginger ale, I'd have loved to have a real drink. We laughed a lot. It was great to be together. And we settled in to work the next day.

The hospital building next to ours was occupied by a native alcohol addiction treatment centre. Up the hill from us was a hospital building also identical to ours. That one was vacant.

It was very quiet. No sounds of Summer School. No great music in the air, no bagpipe player piping his rounds in the morning, no teenagers laughing and rushing to classes, musicians of every ilk. The professional musicians at the school were happy people, laughing together and making wonderful music, compared to writers, shut up alone in our little rooms with only words for company. And those coming some days more readily than others.

One summer a Scottish bagpiper reputed the best in the world was there. As was Mrs. Florence James, 81 years old, and one of the founders of the school. She asked if I would go with her to hear the piper play in Darke Hall, in Regina. She said being the best in the world deserved an audience. Around and around the big room he played, not a centimeter of difference in his solemn footsteps, and after a particularly long piece Mrs. James turned to me and said, Silly looking instrument, isn't it? just as the piece ended abruptly, her words clear to all.

Another bagpiper story. A Scottish piper hired to teach at the Summer School was picked up and lodged in the musicians' residence the night before most others arrived. In the morning he was gone, leaving a note to say, Sorry, I can't stand the vibes here, and back to Scotland he went. Ghost stories about the hospital abounded.

This retreat was quiet. We got together over meals in the dining rooms and evening get-togethers for drinks and encouragement, and the odd visit in the lounge when you took a break in the day, but the same energy wasn't in the air. And with the advent of computers there wasn't even the clatter of typewriters – I missed that – just the occasional swear word and laughter rippling down the hall.

A couple of days in, people started sharing strange experiences. Sudden very cold spots in a room. The feel of a presence in the room making your heart pound. I had not felt anything strange but believed others did. Especially the poor guy whose room was next to the lounge. It was ice cold in places, one corner in particular. People who had crucifixes hung them on the head of their beds. I fashioned one from twigs.

Then one night people woke at 2 a.m. to loud crashing sounds from the kitchen, like crockery smashing. People got up to see empty shelves, the evidence on the floor. That was freakish. And scary, since no one in the building would have gotten up in the night to smash dishes.

I went over to say hello at the treatment centre next door. The nice guy in charge offered me a coffee and we visited.

Have you folks next door noticed anything strange over there? he asked. I told him what had happened and he nodded. Oh yes, he said. People check in here for treatment, and the next morning they are three in the bed.

And you know that building up the hill from you? One night a few people who couldn't sleep got together to talk. They said that the building up the hill was all lit up and there were doctors and nurses moving around something draped in white on a table. They all swore they saw the same thing. A couple of them left the next day.

I'm surprised they all didn't, I said. He laughed. They're just spirits, he said, like he might say they're just people. I hoped my goosebumps didn't show. But we may have to find another place for the centre, he said. Someone later said they did.

A meeting was called to exchange stories and to discuss how best to deal with the situation in our building. It was agreed (not unanimously) that a restless spirit was trying to make contact and maybe if it could the happenings would stop. It was decided that Kate and Patrick would make an ouija, commonly called a weejie board, and we would meet in the lounge at seven the next evening.

We dribbled in before seven, a rather sober lot not knowing what to expect.

The weejie board, with numbers one to nine around the circumference, was on a small table where Patrick and Kate seated across from each other. The words "Yes" and "No" on paper were placed on the board. I don't remember what they used for a planchette, and did they each have one? I'd never seen a weejie board session before and don't remember that.

When everyone was gathered around the room Patrick said we must have complete silence in the room. Scared silent, some of us, a couple of raised eyebrows and some eye rolling. But not for long.

I need to say that I may not remember every word but most of them, and am sure of the questions asked, and the responses.

When all was silent Patrick asked, Is there someone on the other side who wishes to make contact with us? The planchette moved. *Y E S*

Can you tell us your name?

It spelled out *T O M.*

Your name is Tom? Kate asked.

Y E S

Were you a patient here?

Y E S

 How did you die?

Patrick and Kate sharing questions.

T B

Answers coming fast now. Urgent.

Are you angry, Tom? Patrick asked.

Y E S ! The paper almost flew. Some muffled screams, mine one of them. Oh God, this was getting scary. Patrick retrieved the paper.

Is there someone you would like to contact?

Y E S Calmer now.

Who do you want to contact?

G E R T R U D E

We all looked at Gertrude Story.

Is Gertrude in this room?

N O

Who is Gertrude?

M Y W I F E

Where did Gertrude die?

H E R E

Was she a patient here?

Y E S

She died of TB?

NO!

The paper flew off the table.

What did she die of?

E X

X rays? One of them asked.

N O!!

What did she die of?

E X P E R The word forming fast...

IMENTS!

Experiments.

A whoosh of electric air swept the room. The hair on my arms went up. I don't recall exactly what happened next but seem to remember Patrick commiserating with Tom, saying how terrible that was and how sorry we were.

And then Tom's responses getting weaker. And finally he was gone.

Reader Alert: There are differing descriptions about the details of what happened that night and I can only give you what I perceived to be true.

And the events actually took place over two nights with the weejie, having been led astray the first night about who Gertrude was. Gertrude Story, we thought, and she gamely prepared herself to receive a message. What she experienced in the night was the intense fragrance of flowers and a sense of peace.

Also the questions and answers leading up to the climax went on longer, but these are the ones I remember. However, there was no disagreement about Tom's presence in the lounge that night. About his story.

Talking about it later, we liked to think that he felt some peace. That he could move on from the site of so much pain. Kate Bitney was great. To her it seemed natural. Her mother, Anne Szumigalski, had long felt a small presence in the Connaught Place house trying to tell her something. One night when her daughters were in a dance performance at their school a woman asked Anne if she lived at 9 Connaught Place. She said the family who had lived there before had a small daughter they treated cruelly. Just her, not the other children. When neighbours saw them leave, that child was not with them, and she'd heard she was not in their new home.

Anne knew now what the small presence wanted

her to know, and told her that she was a part of their family now and they loved her. And she seemed to know and was at peace.

What happened at that retreat has stayed with those who were there. I have heard, but have no proof, that patients were experimented on but it seems likely.

If anyone asks me if I believe in spirits I say I do. Besides, a couple of friends have told me about their mothers speaking to them shortly after, or at the moment of their passing in another place. One described her mother sitting on her bed, the other standing at the end of the bed. I believe them.

The retreat settled down, I can't remember any other ghostly experiences there but can't really remember. But it was hard to settle down after that night, and getting ready to leave that place felt very good.

Scott, Anne, daughter-in-law Gina and Odell. Mom and me and Teddy. Leona took the picture.

What I'm Trying to Say is Goodbye

I wanted to write about a child who fell in love with words in grade four but was almost forty before her dream to write was realized.

When I thought of writing a memoir starting with "I was born in Edam, Saskatchewan in 1932" and plodding on from there, it always made me feel tired.

It was not until I thought of doing just the events I never forgot, because of some emotional attachment, perhaps – the funny, the scary, the sad, and the downright weird – that I got excited about doing it. Perhaps it would encourage other late starters, and if so, that's good, but that's not why I wrote it. It was partly from guilt about forgetting to write about our family in the Livelong Legacy history book. Obviously that would have been easier.

I didn't intend to make this book so personal. But that's what life is, isn't it? It's personal. And leaving great gaps in the story out of the fear of being judged didn't make sense to me. It's mine and I own it all.

One of my fairly long school trips was to Christopher Lake School, north of Prince Albert. I had a good time with the great kids there.

Thank you letters arrived. They all started the same. *I really enjoyed your visit to Christopher Lake School,* obviously written on the blackboard for them to copy. After that they were on their own.

A grade four boy went on like this: *It was nice of you to come all the way from Saskatoon to Christopher Lake School because from Saskatoon to Prince Albert is 141 kilometers, and from Prince Albert to Christopher Lake is 40 kilometers, and from Christopher Lake to Christopher Lake School is what I'm trying to say is goodbye.*

Saying goodbye is hard sometimes. It is now.

Thank you to all my readers, especially children. I love you all.

ACKNOWLEDGMENTS

My heartfelt thanks to the Saskatchewan Writers Guild and its founders, Ken Mitchell and many others. Without it I doubt I would have become a writer.

An earlier version of this manuscript won second prize in the SWG's 2017 John V. Hicks Long Manuscript Award for nonfiction, and I am grateful.

Thanks to Coteau Books, the wonderful brainchild of Geoffrey Ursell, Barbara Sapergia, Bob Currie and the late Gary Hyland.

I'm so grateful to dee Hobsbawn-Smith for the smart, insightful, no-stone-left-unturned editing job. And her generous support of a temporarily burned-out writer. Thank you from my heart, dee. You made my book so much better.

Thank you to the Saskatchewan Arts Board for the great Summer School of the Arts, and for its support.

And thanks for the memories, everyone.

ABOUT THE AUTHOR

Lois Simmie is an author of children's books, adult fiction, a historical true crime story, radio plays and a children's play for live theatre.

Lois lives in Saskatoon, Saskatchewan and has won many awards for her published works, including the Saskatchewan Writers Guild's Literary Award for Fiction, The Saskatchewan Book Award for Children's Literature and the Crime Writers of Canada's Arthur Ellis Award.